HE THAT COMETH

The Birth of Jesus in the New Testament

HE THAT COMETH

The Birth of Jesus in the New Testament

Reginald H. Fuller

MOREHOUSE PUBLISHING
Harrisburg, PA • Wilton, CT

©1990 by Reginald H. Fuller

All rights reserved. No part of this book may be reproduced, stored in a retrieval system, or transmitted in any form or by any means, electronic, mechanical, photocopying, recording, or otherwise, without the written permission of the publisher.

Morehouse Publishing

Editorial Office
78 Danbury Road
Wilton, CT 06897

Corporate Office
P.O. Box 1321
Harrisburg, PA 17105

Library of Congress Cataloging-in-Publication Data
Fuller, Reginald Horace.
  He that cometh : the birth of Jesus in the New Testament /
Reginald H. Fuller.
    p. cm.
  Includes bibliographical references and index.
  ISBN 0-8192-1544-9
  1. Jesus Christ—Nativity. 2. Jesus Christ—History of doctrines—Early church, ca. 30—600. 3. Bible. N.T.—Criticism. interpretation, etc. I. Title.
BT315.2.F84 1990
232.92'1—dc20   90-39037
                                                                 CIP

Printed in the United States of America
by
BSC Litho
Harrisburg, PA 17105

To Granville Cecil Woods, Jr.,
in gratitude and respect

Contents

Preface

This little book originated in four lectures that were delivered at Christ and Grace Episcopal Church, Petersburg, Virginia, during Advent 1988, under the same title. That title was suggested by the then rector of that church, the Reverend Edwin Lyman Bishop. I am grateful to him for his encouragement and to the congregation for their reception of the lectures.

My idea was to approach the birth of Christ indirectly, seeking first to discover how the other New Testament writers treated that topic before focusing on the birth stories of Matthew and Luke. I have long thought that these stories were expressions of Christology rather than historical narratives. But to regard them as mere fairy stories fails to do justice to their profound christological concern. Of that concern they are a narrative expression.

The dedication to the former president and dean of the Protestant Episcopal Seminary in Virginia is an expression of my gratitude for the happy years in which I taught at that institution under his wise and perceptive leadership and of my respect for him as an embodiment of the best traditions of classical Anglicanism. I hope my insistence on the true humanity of Jesus will be found to be compatible with the classical Anglican doctrine of the incarnation.

Epiphany 1990

1. Jesus' Attitude to His Own Birth

So far as we know, Jesus never told the story of his birth. Early Jesus tradition in the Gospels, however, includes three utterances of Jesus in which he adopts what is apparently a quite negative attitude toward his parentage and family. Two of these passages are found in our earliest Gospel, that according to Mark. In the first of them (Mark 3:20–21, 28–30), Jesus' family appeared on the scene during his Galilean ministry and wanted to 'seize' him. This was because the people were saying, "He is beside himself." There are some problems of translation here. The phrase *his family* literally reads "those from him," i.e., those from his home, like the French *chez lui*. Were they actually family or just acquaintances from back home? The continuation of the story (vv. 31–35) after the intervening Beelzebul controversy (vv. 23–27) suggests that the "people from home" were in fact "his mother and his brothers and his sisters." So RSV is pretty certainly correct in translating "those from him" as "his family."

The second problem is, who was it who was saying that Jesus was "beside himself"? The

1

Greek vaguely mentions "they" were saying. RSV takes this in an indefinite sense, "people" were saying. But it could refer back to "those from him," his family. In either case, however, the motive of Jesus' family in turning up to take him home (?) seems to be that they wanted to stop his public ministry, either because they thought he might harm himself or else because they thought that other people (e.g., his critics) might harm him. In any case, it shows that Jesus' family did not at this time identify with his cause.

Jesus' reaction, when told that his family was outside and presumably had come to fetch him home, was equally negative: " 'Who are my mother and my brothers?' And looking around on those who sat about him (i.e., apparently, his disciples and followers rather than his hostile critics), he said, 'Here are my mother and my brothers! Whoever does the will of God is my brother and sister, and mother.' " This pronouncement, curiously negative in its implication about Jesus' natural family, indicates that, in response to his call to proclaim the coming kingdom of God, Jesus had broken his ties with his natural family and acquired instead a new family consisting of those who had responded positively to his message and had followed him. Jesus' "eschatological" family, as it has been called, has replaced his natural family. He does not, of course, deny that he had a natural mother or natural brothers and sisters (and, therefore, presumably a natural father, who, we may assume since he does not figure in this story, was no longer alive). But Jesus' natural birth cannot provide a full account of his

2

person and mission. In a society in which people's identity was largely determined by their descent and birth, it was expected that a son would follow his father's trade. His ambition would be to become just like his father. This suggests that there are two sides to Jesus: his ancestral and family origin and the breach with that origin that his call necessitated.

The second episode in Mark is of similar negative import. In Mark 6:1–6, we read of Jesus returning to "his own country" (RSV). The Greek word for country is *patris* and means "home town," the ancestral city, presumably Nazareth (Mark 1:9). On this visit, the people of Nazareth rejected Jesus. We are not told that his own family was directly involved in this rejection, only that the people of Nazareth found it hard, if not impossible, to accept him as a prophet whom they had known as a local boy: "Is not this the carpenter, the son of Mary and brother of James and Joses and Judas and Simon, and are not his sisters here with us?"[1] But Jesus goes on to include "his own kin" among those who show him no honor. Here this is another expression of a negative attitude on the part of Jesus toward his own family. Yet again Jesus does not deny that they *are* his own kin, and therefore by implication he admits that Mary was indeed his mother. However, at this point in his life this has only a negative significance for him. His birth provides the appropriate milieu in which the prophetic fate of rejection occurs.

A third synoptic saying, found only in Luke, has some affinity with the first saying in Mark about Jesus' eschatological family. This is Luke

11:27–28. These verses read, "As he said this, a woman in the crowd raised her voice and said to him, 'Blessed is the womb that bore you and the breasts that you sucked.' But he said, 'Blessed rather are those who hear the word of God and keep it!' " This saying occurs at the conclusion of the Q version of the Beelzebul controversy (Luke 11:14–26, parallel Q).[2] For this reason it would be attractive to suppose that the two additional verses, 27 and 28, also come from Q and that Matthew deliberately omitted them because of their implied negative attitude to Jesus' mother. If they are not from Q, they come from Luke's special material (SpL). They are almost identical in import to Mark's saying about Jesus' eschatological family (see above). The combination of the Beelzebul controversy and this type of saying must, therefore, originate from an early stage of the synoptic tradition. In the saying we are discussing, Jesus again suggests that the real relationship to him that matters is for a person to "do the will of God." In this context, to do the will of God means to respond to Jesus' message and to follow him, in other words, to be a disciple and, therefore, to belong to his eschatological family.

These traditions about the family of Jesus are so different from the attitude that later prevailed that their authenticity seems assured. They belong to stage 1 material.[3] A careful examination of these materials shows, however, two sides to them. There is an earthly and a heavenly side to Jesus' person and mission. On the one hand, he was born of an earthly mother and was a member of an earthly family. He had a native town; he was a Jew and a Galilean, a man from Nazareth as we have already seen. On the other hand, he had a mission and a message and assumed a life-style that did not originate in his upbringing but was a response to a call from God. This double–sidedness of Jesus will later find expression in the birth stories.

Was Jesus aware of a tradition that his family was of Davidic descent? Three passages in Mark's Gospel suggest that he was. In the first, he is hailed as the Son of David; in the second he is acclaimed as the restorer of David's kingdom; and in the third he discusses its adequacy as a title of the Messiah.[4] Unfortunately, all three passages are stage 2 materials, that is to say, they do not go back to Jesus himself but originate in the post–Easter community. It is, however, historically probable that there was a tradition of the Davidic descent of Jesus' family. Many years later, members of his family appeared in Rome and claimed royal descent.[5] If Jesus was aware of this tradition, it could have led him to reflect on the prophecies of Isaiah 9 and 11, and these, in turn, would have brought him to Isaiah 35 and 61, which undoubtedly shaped his understanding of his mission. This, however, is only speculation.

2. The Birth of Christ in the Earliest Communities

In a number of places in Paul's letters, he quotes from earlier traditions. These quotations take us back to the thirties and forties of the common era and give us a good idea of the christological kerygma of the earlier communities. In one passage in particular (namely, 1 Cor. 15:3–5), Paul quotes an earlier formula. Here Paul explicitly states that this was a tradition that he passed on to the Corinthians when he first preached in their city but that he received from his predecessors. This must take us back, either to Damascus around the year 33, immediately after Paul's conversion, or to his first visit to Jerusalem after his conversion in the year 35. The formula reads as follows:

> I delivered to you as of first importance what I also received, that Christ died for our sins in accordance with the scriptures, that he was buried, that he was raised on the third day in accordance with the scriptures, and that he appeared . . .

We find nothing here about the birth of Jesus nor, indeed, anything about his earthly life prior to the point of his death. The focus is exclusively upon Jesus' end. Of course, one might argue that Paul was merely being selective, choosing those parts of the tradition that were immediately relevant to his argument in 1 Corinthians. He was arguing about the resurrection of the dead. However, the same exclusive focus upon the end of Jesus' career is found in other places where Paul is harking back to earlier tradition. For instance, in writing to the Thessalonians, the earliest letter we have from his pen, he again reminds them of his initial preaching to which they had responded in faith. This time it reads as follows:

> You turned to God from idols, to serve a living and true God, and to wait for his Son from heaven, whom he raised from the dead, Jesus, who delivers us from the wrath to come. (1 Thess. 1:9)

This time even the death of Jesus is only implied by the reference to his rising from the dead, and the focus is upon his Second Coming. But still there is nothing about the beginning of Jesus' life.

Paul wrote his letter to the Romans to introduce himself to the Christians there, for unlike his other letters, Romans was addressed to a city he had not yet visited. So this time he cannot remind them of his previous preaching but recalls instead traditions that he and other Christian missionaries share and that the Roman Christians would have heard from them. When they were baptized, they made a confession of faith, and Paul reminds them of that confession when he writes:

> The word is near you, on your lips and in your heart (that is, the word of faith which we preach); because, if you confess with your lips that Jesus is Lord and believe in your heart that God raised him from the dead, you will be saved. (Rom. 10:8–9)

Once again, the focus is exclusively on the raising of Jesus from the dead and his enthronement as Lord. His death is obliquely referred to ("God raised him from the dead"). That he had an earthly career is implied by the human name, Jesus. But nothing is said of his birth.

There is, however, one other early formula in Romans, right at the beginning. Paul here speaks about the gospel that he as an apostle had been entrusted to preach. Significantly, he defines that gospel in terms very different from those he normally used. This is because on this occasion he is writing to Christians who had responded to the preaching of other Jewish Christian missionaries. These missionaries formulated the gospel in terms very different from Paul's own. Paul was, of course, a Jew, but there were different groups within the early church. There was a very conservative group around James, a rather less conservative group around Peter, and a radical group around Stephen. It is probable that the Christians Paul is addressing at Rome in this part of his letter belonged to the group associated with Peter. The formula Paul quotes here reads as follows:

> . . . who was descended from David according to the flesh and designated Son of God in power according to the Spirit of

holiness by his resurrection from the
dead. (Rom. 1:3b–4)

The phrase translated by the RSV as "descended
from David" literally translated reads "having
come into being from the seed of David" or "born
of the seed of David." Thus, we have here a
specific reference to the birth of Jesus for the
first time in the pre–Pauline traditions. In other
words, the birth of Jesus does have a christological significance. But we must be quite
clear what this significance is. The formula does
not say that Jesus was Messiah from his birth,
for Davidic descent does not in itself connote
messiahship. After all, Jesus' ancestors were all
descended from David. Rather, Davidic descent
qualifies Jesus for the messianic office that was
conferred upon him by God at the resurrection.
That is what "designated Son of God . . . by his
resurrection from the dead" means. "Son of
God" is here used not in an ontological sense
but to indicate an office or function. The birth of
Jesus in this formula is not in itself a christological moment but the essential precondition
for the supreme christological moment, which is
the resurrection. But in this formula we do find
the starting point of a process that will lead
eventually to the shaping of the birth stories.

The Kerygmatic Speeches in Acts

Other formulae in Paul are of pre–Pauline
origin. But as we shall show later, these
formulae are of later origin than those we have
considered thus far. Let us turn, instead, to the
kerygmatic speeches in Acts. In particular, those
speeches in chapters 2 and 10 are significant for

our purpose. There has been much discussion as to whether these speeches are pre–Lucan in origin or whether they were composed by Luke himself in accordance with the practice of Greek historians from the time of Thucydides. My own view is that, while in their finished form these speeches in Acts are the composition of the author, their christological core is much earlier and can be used as evidence for the Christology of the earliest Jerusalem community.[1]

The first of these speeches, which is put into the mouth of Peter at Pentecost, is focused upon the death and resurrection of Jesus but is prefaced by a brief summary of his activity during the public ministry: "Jesus of Nazareth, a man attested to you by God with mighty works and wonders and signs which God did through him in your midst" (Acts 2:22). The reference to Nazareth does suggest some concern for Jesus' origin, but nothing is said about his birth. The main focus is still upon the death and resurrection of Jesus:

> . . . this Jesus, delivered up according to the definite plan and foreknowledge of God, you crucified and killed by the hands of lawless men. But God raised him up, having loosed the pangs of death, . . . and of that we all are witnesses . . . Let all the house of Israel therefore know assuredly that God has made him both Lord and Christ, this Jesus whom you crucified. (Acts 2:23–24a, 32a, 36)

The resurrection is still the supreme christological moment, as it was in the formula of Rom. 1:3–4. It was at that moment that God "made" him Lord and Christ; as in the Romans formula, appointed him to be Son of God. But the earthly life of Jesus begins to have some preliminary christological significance. Jesus was not just an ordinary human being, for we are told that "God did these mighty works through him." This recognition of christological significance in the earthly life of Jesus prior to his death and resurrection is preparing the way for the later concern with Jesus' birth as an integral element of Christology. Yet we are still a long way from that.

In the second kerygmatic speech, that of Acts 10, this christological concern is taken back a little earlier, to the activity of John the Baptist and to the anointing of Jesus with the Holy Spirit at the outset of his ministry:

> You know the word . . . which was proclaimed throughout all Judea, beginning from Galilee after the baptism which John preached: how God anointed Jesus of Nazareth with the Holy Spirit and with power; how he went about doing good and healing all that were oppressed by the devil, for God was with him. And we are witnesses to all that he did both in the country of the Jews and in Jerusalem. (Acts 10:36a, 37–39a)

While, as the ensuing verses make clear, the death and resurrection of Jesus still form the christological climax, God was with Jesus from the moment he was anointed by the Holy Spirit, presumably from the time of his baptism. This anointing has become an important, though preliminary, christological moment. But the process of retrojection is not yet complete. It is not yet stated that Jesus became Son of God or the Messiah at his baptism. Presumably, although this speech does not explicitly mention it, this occurred when he was "ordained by God to be the judge of the living and the dead" (Acts 10:42b). The speech does not say when this ordination took place, but probably it was at the resurrection.

The Christology of these two speeches varies. But they both agree that the death/resurrection of Jesus is the supreme christological moment. Yet the earthly life is beginning to acquire some preliminary christological significance. This development will lead eventually to a concern with the birth of Jesus.

The Later pre–Pauline Formulae

In Paul's Letter to the Galatians, we have a formula that represents a further development. It reads as follows:

> God sent forth his Son, born of woman
> . . . so that we might receive adoption as
> sons. (Gal. 4:4–5)

Paul has expanded this formula to include a reference to Christ's being "born under the law, to redeem those who were under the law." These words represent Paul's particular theological interest and were not part of the original formula. We shall consider them in a later chapter. The pre–Pauline nucleus represents the earliest example we have of the so–called sending formula.[2] This formula has a regular pattern: a verb of sending, with God as the subject and the Son as the object, together with a purpose clause denoting the soteriological or saving purpose of that sending. This sending formula represents a decisive shift of the christological moment from the end to the beginning of Jesus' course, from the resurrection to the inception of his mission. The phrase "born of woman" has suggested to many scholars that the christological moment in question was that of Jesus' birth. In addition, it has been thought that "born of woman" is intended to imply the virginal conception, as though Jesus was born of a woman and not of a man, but this can hardly be the meaning. It is said, for instance, in connection with John the Baptist that "among those born of women there has arisen no one greater than" he (Matt. 11:11par.). The phrase simply means a real human being. But apart from that, does the formula imply that the birth of Jesus was the moment of his sending? This is tied up with the further problem of whether the formula intends to assert Christ's heavenly preexistence. That has often been asserted on the grounds that the verb "sent *forth*," which in Greek is a double compound (*ex–ap–esteilen*, literally, "sent *out from*"), implies that the Son was preexistent and sent forth by God from heaven. While, as we shall see in chapter 4, this is probably how Paul understood the formula, it is doubtful whether this is the original meaning. Taken by itself, the double compound means no more than the ordinary single compound (*apo–stellō*). The double compound form refers in the Septuagint (Greek translation of the Old Testament) to the historical commissioning of the Old Testament (OT) prophets, as for instance in Amos 1:4. The prophets did not claim to be preexistent, nor did they regard their birth as the moment of their commissioning. This is clear when Isaiah responds to his call with the words "Here am I! Send me" (Isa. 6:8). The historical Jesus spoke in similar terms of his commissioning: "Whoever receives me, receives not me but him who sent me" (Mark 9:37b). He also compared his mission with an owner of a vineyard sending his beloved son to collect the rent from the tenants (Mark 12:6). Thus, in origin the whole concept of sending referred not to preexistence and birth but to historical commissioning. In Jesus' own thinking it was tied up with his prophetic self–consciousness. We do not know for certain, but quite probably the earliest community continued after Easter to speak of Jesus as the last and greatest of the prophets sent by God. In the course of time, however, the title *Son* was retrojected from the moment of the resurrection to the moment of Jesus' baptism. This development has already occurred in the Gospel accounts of the baptism of Jesus in which the voice from heaven declares him to be God's Son (Mark 1:11 parallels). Some scholars have thought that in the earlier tradition the voice from heaven declared Jesus to be his servant (a term denoting a prophetic figure rather than son). If this is so, a development has taken place in which the title *Son* has been retrojected from the resurrection to the baptism of Jesus. The formula in Gal. 4:4 attests to this development. God sent forth his Son, not at his birth but at his baptism. But this development does prepare the way for its further retrojection to the moment of the birth, as we shall see when we come to consider Paul's reinterpretation of this formula in chapter 4.

A more developed pre–Pauline Christology is evidenced in the well–known hymn in Phil. 2:6–11:

> . . . who, though he was in the form of God,
> did not count equality with God a thing
>   to be grasped,
> but emptied himself,
> taking the form of a servant,
> being born in the likeness of men.
> And being found in human form
> he humbled himself
> and became obedient unto death. . . .
> Therefore God has highly exalted him
> and bestowed on him the name which is
>   above every name,
> that at the name of Jesus every knee
>   should bow,
> in heaven and under the earth,
> and every tongue confess
> that Jesus Christ is Lord,
> to the glory of God the Father.

The pre–Pauline origin of this hymn is almost universally accepted. But there is some dispute among scholars as to whether it expresses a two– or three–step Christology. If it is the former, it represents Christ as the One who was born as the last Adam. Like the first Adam, he was "in the form of God," i.e., made in the divine image. Unlike the first Adam, however, he did not grasp at equality with God ("you shall be like God," Gen. 3:5). Instead, he lived a life of self–emptying, following the pattern of a servant's life. The phrase being "born in the likeness of men" will then refer, not to a further stage in self–emptying, but resumes what has been stated thus far and functions as a kind of parenthesis. The story then continues to speak of Christ as the last Adam who, being in human form like the first Adam, humbled himself to the point of death. As a result of his obedience, which canceled out the disobedience of the first Adam, God exalted him and bestowed on him the name that is above every name. In the three-step interpretation, the Redeemer preexisted as the divine wisdom in the form of God, i.e., in the divine mode of being or in the divine glory. He did not, however, cling to this mode of existence or divine glory but divested himself and assumed the form of a slave or servant in a human birth. After becoming incarnate, he humbled himself even further and, in a life of obedience, submitted to death. In both inter-pretations, the birth of the Redeemer constitutes a decisive christological moment. The majority opinion favors the three–step interpretation, and we agree. The phrase "being born in the likeness of men" occurs after the phrase "emptied himself" and implies a further stage of the way of the Redeemer. It, therefore, makes much better sense to interpret this hymn as the earliest expression we have of a preexis-tence/incarnation Christology in which the birth marks the decisive moment of the incarnation. At the same time the birth is not the climactic christological moment but only a stage in the self-humiliation of the Redeemer on the way to death. The decisive christological moment remains his exaltation as the Redeemer in which he received the name of Lord (*kyrios,* the name of Yahweh himself in Hellenistic Greek usage). In short, the main focus is still on the end rather than on the beginning of the way of the Redeemer.

Summary and Conclusion

The kerygma of the earliest Christians focused exclusively upon the death and resurrection of Jesus. The resurrection was the decisive christological moment, the moment when Jesus was appointed the Christ (Messiah), Lord, and Son of God. Some forms of this kerygma prefaced the recital of Jesus' death and resurrection with a succinct summary of his earthly career, which was not entirely devoid of christological significance. God was active in Jesus' history. In other circles, the birth of Jesus became important because his Davidic descent qualified him for the messianic office to which he was appointed at the resurrection. Somewhat later, the sending formula was developed. This stressed the divine initiative at the beginning of Jesus' career, though its climax was the soteriological purpose that would be accomplished at the end of his earthly life. Another development was the three–step Christology in which the preexistent One became incarnate in a human birth that was the necessary prelude to his death and exaltation. All these developments contribute to a shift of christological concern from the end to the beginning of Jesus' life. In one way or another, all of them, with the exception of the incarnation pattern, will contribute to the Christologies expressed in the birth narratives of Matthew and Luke.

3. The Birth of Christ in Mark and Q

We have already looked at some of the relevant passages in Mark when discussing Jesus' own attitude to his birth. In this chapter, we are concerned with Mark's own attitude to the birth of Jesus as an aspect of his Christology.

By incorporating the Davidic materials and those traditions in which Jesus contrasts his earthly family with his eschatological family, Mark shows at the very minimum that he was aware of Jesus' human birth. But the focus of the earliest evangelist's christological concern is not upon the birth of Jesus but, like the earliest kerygma, upon his death and resurrection. Mark shows this in a number of different ways. He begins the narrative of Jesus' earthly ministry, not with his birth, but with the prior ministry of John the Baptist, leading to the baptism of Jesus himself. In this, Mark is following exactly the same procedure as the kerygmatic speech attributed to Peter in Acts 10. After the narrative of Jesus' baptism, Mark seems to rush breathlessly to get to the Passion. This is indicated by his frequent use of the word *immediately* (Greek: *euthys*). It is as if Mark cannot wait until he gets to the cross. From the moment of Jesus' baptism, when he was designated as Son of God by a voice from heaven, "thou art my beloved Son; with thee I am well pleased (1:11)," the shadow of the cross looms over Mark's story. The voice from heaven we have just quoted is a combined quotation of Ps. 2:7 and Isa. 42:1. This qualifies Jesus' divine sonship in terms of the Servant of Yahweh in deutero–Isaiah and so opens up the prospect of suffering. When the Pharisees question Jesus about the disciples' omission of the practice of fasting, he predicts that "the days will come when the bridegroom is taken away from them" (Mark 2:20). A little later we are told that "the Pharisees went out and immediately held counsel with the Herodians against him, how to destroy him" (Mark 3:6). From chapter 8 onward, the narrative is punctuated with a series of passion predictions that have been likened to the tolling of a bell:

the Son of man must suffer many things, and be rejected by the elders and the chief priests and the scribes, and be killed, and after three days rise again. (Mark 8:31)

how is it written of the Son of man, that he should suffer many things and be treated with contempt? (Mark 9:12)

The Son of man will be delivered into the hands of men, and they will kill him; and when he is killed, after three days he will rise (Mark 9:31)

Behold, we are going up to Jerusalem; and the Son of man will be delivered to the chief priests and the scribes, and they will condemn him to death and deliver him to the Gentiles; and they will mock him, and spit upon him, and scourge him, and kill him; and after three days he will arise. (Mark 10:33–34)

. . . the Son of man also came not to be served but to serve, and to give his life as a ransom for many. (Mark 10:45)

In addition to these passion predictions, there are other places where Jesus refers to his impending death. Thus, he speaks of the cup he is to drink and the baptism he is to undergo (Mark 10:39). This passage reinforces the significance of Jesus' baptism by John as a foreshadowing of his death. Finally, the parable of the vineyard culminates in the killing of the heir by the tenants (Mark 12:8).

Nearly all of these sayings focus exclusively upon the end of Jesus, his rejection, suffering, death, and resurrection. In this respect they correspond to the earliest kerygma as we have seen it in 1 Cor. 15:3–5. There are, however, two exceptions. In Mark 10:45, we read that the Son of man "came," followed by a statement of soteriological purpose. Similarly, the parable of the vineyard speaks of the owner "sending" his son. Some interpreters have thought that Mark already has a preexistence/incarnation Christology and have so interpreted, not only these two passages, but also Mark 1:38 ("Let us go on to the next towns, that I may preach there also; for that is why I came out"). The word translated "came out" could also be taken to mean "came forth," i.e., from heaven. It is most unlikely, however, that Mark has Christology of this type. He almost certainly means that Christ's sending and coming was a this–worldly historical event. That event was his commissioning at his baptism and the inauguration of his historical mission. This means that Mark's Christology has reached the same point of development we find in the sending formula of Gal. 4:4. This would be consistent with his major focus upon the end of Jesus rather than upon his beginning. In the last analysis, the reason for his commission was that he should die upon the cross. There is no reference to the birth of Jesus in these allusions to his sending and his coming.

A well–known feature of Mark is the device we call the *messianic secret*. This expresses itself in a number of different ways, some of which may be historical, others traditional, and yet others redactional, though all of them are used by Mark in the interests of his christological purpose. When Jesus performs exorcisms, the demons cry out, "I know who you are, the Holy One of God" (Mark 1:24), or some similar christological acclamation. When this happens, Jesus silences them. In healing miracles, Jesus sometimes commands the healed person or the witnesses to remain silent about the cure (e.g., Mark 5:43). Sometimes Jesus takes a sick person aside and heals that person privately (e.g., Mark 7:33). On other occasions, Jesus teaches his disciples alone, away from the crowd (e.g. Mark 4:10–20). At Caesarea Philippi, when Peter acknowledges Jesus to be the Messiah, Jesus at once commands the disciples to tell no one about it

(Mark 8:30). Most important of all, when Peter, James, and John come down from the mountain of Transfiguration, Jesus tells them to keep quiet about their experience until after the Son of man should have risen from the dead (Mark 9:9). Only in the context of his Passion does Jesus answer the high priest's question, "Are you the Messiah?" with a bold "I am." Finally, only after Jesus' death, does the centurion publicly proclaim, "Truly, this man was the Son of God."

The meaning of the messianic secret has been much discussed. The solution probably lies in Mark's theology of the cross. If Jesus had been publicly acknowledged during his earthly life or had proclaimed himself as such, this would have suggested that the Messiah was merely a miracle worker. For Mark, it is only the crucified One who is the Messiah. This theology of the cross has implications for the birth of Jesus in Mark's theology. Had Mark narrated that birth, he would have had to disclose the messianic secret from the very beginning, as happened later in the birth stories of Matthew and Luke. A birth story would thus have been inconsistent with Mark's theology of the cross.

We have already mentioned that Mark incorporates passages about Jesus' Davidic descent. Let us now turn to his redactional treatment of this theme. In the healing of Bartimaeus, Jesus is hailed by the blind man as Son of David (Mark 10:46–52) as he cries to Jesus for help. When Jesus has healed him, Bartimaeus follows Jesus "on the way," by which Mark means the way to the cross. For Mark, therefore, Son of David is not a title with an intrinsic value but has only provisional significance. As Son of David, Jesus grants deliverance from the blindness that cannot see in him the One who goes to the cross and calls others to follow him on that way.

The second Davidic passage is the entry into Jerusalem on Palm Sunday (Mark 11:1–10). In Mark's version (unlike Matthew's), Jesus is not directly hailed as Son of David. Rather, as he approaches Jerusalem, the crowd acclaims the coming of the "kingdom of our father David." As Günther Bornkamm has rightly observed, this story has been "messianically overexposed" in the post–Easter tradition. At the historical level (stage 1), the crowd was merely singing Psalm 118 to welcome the arrival of the pilgrims generally, Jesus included. The later community will have added the words about the kingdom of our father David in the light of its post–Easter faith. "Our father" was never used of David in Judaism and reflects the Christian community's belief that Jesus was the Son of David. Curiously, Mark's story ends in an anticlimax. Jesus, as Eduard Schweizer has remarked, simply looks around the Temple "like a tourist." For Mark, the story awaits its conclusion in the death and resurrection of Jesus. Only then is the kingdom of "our father David" inaugurated. In no way does Mark exploit the triumphal entry so as to throw light on Jesus' Davidic birth. Matthew and Luke, on the other hand, make the crowds explicitly acknowledge Jesus as the Son of David or king of Israel. For both Matthew and Luke, the crowd acclaims Jesus as he was designated already in their birth narratives. Moreover, Luke deliberately replaces the hosanna with "peace in heaven and glory in the highest," thus obviously echoing the angels' hymn at the birth of Jesus. Such connections would have been totally contrary to the messianic secret in Mark.

The third passage in which the Son of David Christology is featured in Mark is the question Jesus addresses to his opponents about how David's son can be David's Lord (Mark 12:35–37). We did not consider this passage when we were discussing the historical Jesus in chapter 1 because it is generally regarded as stage 2 material, i.e., as a creation of the post–Easter community. This view of its origin is probably correct, for it reflects the church's belief in the lordship of Jesus after his resurrection. At first sight it looks as though Jesus is rejecting the view that the Messiah is the Son of David: "David himself calls him Lord; so how is he his son?" It is, however, hard to believe that any early Christian writer would have dismissed the tradition of Jesus' Davidic descent. Rather, the point must be that the exalted Messiah is more than that. He is David's Lord. The title Son of David is not wrong but inadequate to express the transcendent status of Jesus after his vindication. The Christology of the passage in question is thus identical with that of the pre-Pauline formula in Rom. 1:3–4, which was discussed in chapter 2. There the title Son of David applied to what Jesus was in the flesh, i.e., his earthly life, while *kyrios* (Lord) indicated what he became in the Spirit.

As we have already noted, Mark takes over the traditions that portray Jesus' earthly family in a negative light (Mark 3:20–21, 31–35;

6:1–6a). He even seems to exaggerate the negative impression of Jesus' family in the first of these two episodes by means of his "sandwich technique." For Mark inserts the Beelzebul controversy between the two parts of the story of Jesus' relatives. Mark seems to make the family of Jesus as bad as the scribes who accuse Jesus of being in league with Beelzebul and, therefore, guilty of the unforgivable sin of blasphemy against the Holy Spirit. But there is a difference. Jesus' family only misunderstood him. They were trying to stop him from pursuing a course that would lead him eventually to the cross. The hostility of the scribes evokes the fears of Jesus' family, not their emulation. Mark is open to the possibility that Jesus' relatives, like the disciples, will eventually come around and understand him after his death and resurrection. If that happens, they too, like the disciples, will become part of Jesus' eschatological family. This is, in fact, what happened historically. James the brother of the Lord later became the leader of the Jerusalem church, while according to Luke (Acts 1:14), Mary the Mother of Jesus makes her last appearance in the New Testament among the disciples waiting after the Ascension for the coming of the Spirit at Pentecost. Mark's treatment of Jesus' family is similar in purport to the messianic secret. It points to the cross and resurrection as the decisive christological moment. Had Mark included a birth story in his Gospel, Jesus' family would have understood him, and this would have compromised the centrality of the cross in Mark's overall scheme.

The Q Material

As the reader will recall, Q is the symbol used to denote the materials common to Matthew and Luke but not found in Mark.[1] These traditions consist almost exclusively of sayings of Jesus. There was no passion narrative in Q and, of course, no birth narrative. Q contains no Son of David materials and nothing about the rejection of Jesus by his family. Q begins with the ministry of John the Baptist, while the next section, which covers the temptation of Jesus, assumes that Jesus is already designated Son of God. Apparently for Q, Jesus was appointed as Son of God at his baptism. It is indeed possible that Q contained a narrative of the baptism, for there are some minor agreements between Matthew and Luke at this point.[2] In any case, Q represents a stage of development in Christology in which the messianic titles are being retrojected from the exaltation to the earthly life of Jesus to the beginning rather than the end of his career. Although Q has nothing about Jesus' birth, it witnesses to a development that is going to lead ultimately to the composition of the birth stories.

For Q, Jesus in his earthly life was the lowly Son of man. He "has nowhere to lay his head" (Matt. 8:20 par.). He "came eating and drinking" (Matt. 11:19 par.). Such a use of Son of man indicates the humanity and human weakness of Jesus and, therefore, implies his human birth. But when Q says that he "came," this will refer not to his birth but to the inception of his mission at his baptism.

The other major Christology in Q presents

Jesus as the final spokesperson of God's Wisdom. There are four or possibly five such sayings in Q. The first of these is the so-called justification saying: "wisdom is justified by all her children" (Luke 7:35 par.). In this saying, Jesus appears as the last of Wisdom's "children" or envoys after John the Baptist, who was the next to last. The second saying is the cry of jubilation (Matt. 11:25–27 par.). Here Jesus says, "All things have been delivered to me by my Father; and no one knows the Son except the Father, and no one knows the Father except the Son and anyone to whom the Son chooses to reveal him." At first sight, this saying seems to be an expression of Father/Son Christology. But when it says that the Father has endowed the Son with "all things" and that the Son reveals knowledge of the Father to others, these are Wisdom motifs. For Wisdom is supremely the agent of God's self–communication.

It is uncertain whether the saying that immediately follows in Matthew (11:28–30) comes from Q since it is absent from Luke. Probably it was included in the form of Q known to Matthew (Q^{Mt}). This is the well–known "comfortable word":

> Come to me, all who labor and are heavy laden, and I will give you rest. Take my yoke upon you, and learn from me; for I am gentle and lowly in heart, and you will find rest for your souls. For my yoke is easy, and my burden is light.

A glance at two passages in the Apocrypha, Ecclesiasticus (Sirach) 24:19 and 51:23–27, will show that Jesus is uttering these words in the name of Wisdom. In the first of these two passages, Wisdom issues the same invitation, "Come to me," and a similar promise of refreshment. In the second passage, we have another invitation and a promise that Wisdom will give rest to those who put their neck under her yoke and receive her instruction. It is quite possible that, in the pre–Gospel tradition, the comfortable word was prefaced with the introduction, "Wisdom says." It is even conceivable that Jesus introduced the invitation in this way. There is no reason why it should not in this form be an authentic saying of the historical Jesus. At some stage in the transmission, either in Q^Mt or in the Evangelist's own redaction, the introductory "Wisdom says" will have been omitted, leaving the saying as a personal invitation of Jesus himself. As we shall see, this is precisely what happened in another one of the Wisdom sayings (Matt. 23:34–35). For Matthew, the result is that Jesus becomes, not simply the spokesperson, but the actual embodiment of Wisdom herself. This is not a full-blown doctrine of incarnation such as would require an allusion to the birth of Jesus as the moment when that incarnation took place. But it does mean that Jesus incarnates the heavenly Wisdom in his ministry, a process that probably began at his baptism. It thus opens up the road to an eventual full–blown doctrine of the incarnation. This important feature of the Q material has often been overlooked.[3]

The fourth Wisdom saying from Q reads as follows:

> Therefore I send you prophets and wise men and scribes, some of whom you will kill and crucify, and some you will scourge in your synagogues and persecute from town to town, that upon you may come all the righteous blood shed on earth, from the blood of innocent Abel to the blood of Zechariah the son of Barachiah, whom you murdered between the sanctuary and the altar. (Matt. 23:34–35)

This is the saying that in the Lucan version (Luke 11:49–50) is explicitly introduced as a saying of Wisdom: "Therefore the Wisdom of God said." The theme, Israel's constant rejection of the prophets throughout her salvation history, is a characteristic Wisdom theme. Jesus is clearly speaking in the Lucan form as the spokesperson of Wisdom, but in the Matthean form he becomes the personal embodiment of Wisdom. Jesus incarnates the heavenly Wisdom who was active in Israel's history from the beginning to the end of the OT, from Abel in the Book of Genesis to Zechariah in 2 Chron. 24:20–22, which would be the last book of the OT in the time of Jesus. Here Matthew comes closest to a preexistence/incarnation Christology. Once again, Jesus presumably began to incarnate Wisdom at the inception of his ministry.

The fifth Wisdom saying is the Jerusalem word in Matt. 23:37–39 par. It reads as follows:

> O Jerusalem, Jerusalem, killing the prophets and stoning those who are sent to you! How often would I have gathered

your children together as a hen gathers her brood under her wings, and you would not.

In both versions of the saying, Matthew's and Luke's, these words appear as a saying of Jesus himself. But they contain typical Wisdom themes: the sending of envoys to Israel throughout her salvation history, the constant invitation to be "gathered," and Israel's constant rejection of Wisdom's envoys.

The effect of these Wisdom sayings from Q is to shift some of the focus from the end of Jesus' career to its beginning. But the shift is never complete. Although Jesus became Wisdom's last envoy and embodiment at the beginning of his ministry, his mission is not accomplished until his final rejection. Thus, the Q material is open at both ends. It points both to the initial sending of Jesus and to the final outcome of his mission in his rejection and Crucifixion. The inner logic of Q is to require completion with the birth story at one end and the Passion at the other, and this is precisely what Matthew and Luke have provided. They embedded Q in Gospels that begin with a birth story and end with Christ's death and resurrection.

4. Paul: Preexistence and Incarnation

From a chronological point of view it would have been more appropriate to discuss Paul before dealing with Mark and Q. Paul's letters were written in the fifties and possibly early sixties, while Mark was written around the year 70. The date of Q is uncertain but possibly contemporaneous with Paul's letters. However, Paul's Christology represents an advance on that of Mark and Q, so we are dealing with Paul at this point.

In this chapter we shall concentrate on those letters whose Pauline authorship is unquestioned, leaving aside those whose authorship is open to doubt.[1]

As we saw in chapter 2, Paul utilized three types of tradition in which the birth of Jesus figures as a christological moment. The three traditions are Davidic descent, the sending formula, and the (probably) three-step Christology in Phil. 2:6–11. We shall now explore the ways in which Paul himself has modified or developed these traditions.

Davidic Descent

Paul introduces the formula in Rom. 1:3–4 with

the statement that it is the tradition concerning "his Son," i.e., the Son of God. As we saw, the formula itself dates Christ's divine sonship from the moment of his exaltation. This means that, for Paul, Christ was already the Son of God before he assumed Davidic descent. Thus, for Paul the birth of Christ becomes the moment of his Incarnation, and a doctrine of preexistence is apparently presumed. There is no specific discussion of this change, but a three-step Christology appears to be taken for granted.

In Rom. 9:5, Paul enumerates the privileges of Israel under the old covenant. One of these privileges is that the Christ (Messiah) belongs to Israel "according to the flesh." This phrase seems to echo the formula of Rom. 1:3–4. If we read Rom. 9:5 in the light of Paul's extension to the pre-Pauline formula in Romans 1:3–4 to cover preexistence and incarnation, we may perhaps interpret the phrase "Messiah according to the flesh" to imply preexistence here, too.

There is one other text in Paul that contains a reference to Jesus' genealogy. This occurs in a citation of Isa. 11:10 at Rom. 15:12. The passage reads as follows:

> The root of Jesse shall come,
> he who rises to rule the Gentiles;
> in him shall the Gentiles hope.

This text was treated as a messianic prophesy in rabbinic Judaism and was probably already regarded as such before the rise of Christianity. Quite independently of Paul, "Root of David" appears as a christological title in Rev. 5:5 and 22:16. It is probable that Paul took this text from a collection of early Christian testimonia

34

(i.e., OT texts that were interpreted as prophecies of Jesus' Davidic descent). Paul himself was not interested in this aspect of the text but used it because it served his immediate purpose of emphasizing the universality of the gospel. The lordship of Christ and the Christian mission are to encompass the Gentiles as well as Israel. As a title, "Root of Jesse" was destined to play a minor role in later Christian lore about the birth of Jesus.

The Seed of Abraham

In Gal. 3:16, Paul indulges in a remarkable piece of rabbinical argumentation:

> The promises were made to Abraham and to his offspring. It does not say, "And to offsprings," referring to many; but referring to one, "And to your offspring," which is Christ.

This line of thought is hardly calculated to convince the modern reader. Paul is basing his argument on Gen. 12:7 and 22:17–18, where God promises a blessing on Abraham's descendants. The Hebrew in these pages refers to Abraham's "seed," as the KJV translates it, and it is quite clear to us that "seed" is meant collectively. We are familiar with this usage in the Magnificat, which speaks of "Abraham and his seed for ever." Paul takes the collective as a singular and construes it as a reference to Christ. We can agree that the promises to Abraham reach their final fulfillment in the person of Jesus and in the blessings that flow from his redemptive act. For our purpose, we

may note that the argument presumes that
Jesus was born as a descendant of Abraham.
This idea is not unique to Paul, for both
Matthew and Luke trace the genealogy of Jesus
from (or, in the case of Luke, up to) Abraham.
Paul thus gives us a glimpse into the workshop
in which the infancy narratives were being
constructed.

It is possible that Paul gives us another
glimpse into this workshop. In Gal. 4:21–31, he
develops a complicated allegory about
Abraham's two sons: Ishmael, who was born of
the slave girl Hagar, and Isaac, the son of the
free woman Sarah. The two children symbolize
for Paul the communities of the old and new
convenants respectively. Isaac, says Paul, was
born according to promise (Gal. 4:23) and
according to the Spirit (Gal. 4:28). Philo of
Alexandria constructs quite a different allegory
on the birth of Abraham's two sons but, like
Paul, makes a particular point of the mode of
Isaac's birth. It has been argued that both Paul
and Philo are dependent upon a Hellenistic
Jewish exegesis of the story of the two sons of
Abraham.[2] The question was posed, How were
Abraham and Sarah able to have a child when
Abraham was a hundred years old and Sarah
ninety? The answer to this conundrum, it was
suggested, was that God by the Holy Spirit
miraculously enabled Sarah to conceive. Similar
conceptions through the Holy Spirit were
suggested for other OT figures. Paul does not
directly allude to this popular midrash but
seems to presuppose it in his allegory. We would
not claim that Paul was familiar with the
doctrine of the virginal conception of Jesus. But

he does seem to be familiar with the midrashic tradition out of which the virginal conception through the Holy Spirit was developed.

The Sending Formula

If it is correct that the core of Gal. 4:4 is a pre-Pauline formula, it spoke of the historical sending of Jesus to perform the role of Son of God and to open up the possibility of adoption as sons of God for the believers. The phrase "born of woman," as we saw, gave no particular emphasis to the fact of Christ's birth but merely asserted his humanity. Paul, however, has expanded the sending formula in the light of his own theological reflections on the law. To the phrase "born of woman," he adds the further remark "born under the law." And to the statement of soteriological purpose, he adds a parallel purpose clause: "to redeem those who were under the law." He has thus given the formula a chiastic structure, *A-B-B-A*:

> God sent forth his Son
> *A* born of woman,
> *B* born under the law
> *B* to redeem those who were under the law,
> *A* so that we might receive adoption as sons.

The effect of this expansion of the original formula for our purposes is twofold. First, the birth of Jesus now becomes a significant christological moment. Unlike "born of woman," "born under the law" refers explicitly to the moment at which the Son of God became subject to the law, i.e., at the moment of birth.

Paul is probably unaware of the stories of Jesus' circumcision and presentation at the Temple as narrated by Luke, but those stories are a narrative expression of the theology Paul enunciates here. This, in turn, gives a new twist to the phrase "born of woman," for this now must refer explicitly to the moment of his birth. Second, the verb "sent forth" must now mean sent from heaven. It implies a doctrine of preexistence and incarnation. Those who argue that the verb "sent forth" means "sent forth from heaven" are correct for the stage of Pauline redaction, even if they are wrong at the level of the pre-Pauline formula.

Our proposed interpretation of the sending formula in the Pauline redaction of Gal. 4:4–5 is corroborated by another occurrence of the sending formula in Rom. 8:3–4. This reads as follows:

> God has done what the law, weakened by the flesh, could not do: sending his own Son in the likeness of sinful flesh and for sin, he condemned sin in the flesh, in order that the just requirement of the law might be fulfilled in us.

It is easy to determine Paul's redactional elements in this formula. The references to the law and to the flesh in its weakness and sinfulness will obviously come from his pen. The original pre-Pauline formula, however, is harder to determine. It must have begun with the statement that God sent his own Son. But where is the statement of soteriological purpose? It probably lies hidden in the phrase "for sin." The RSV margin suggests an alternative translation: "as a sin offering." The Greek phrase literally means "concerning sin" (*peri hamartias*). But it is commonly used in the OT to translate the technical term in Hebrew for "sin offering." It occurs in this sense in Heb. 10:6 and 8. In verse 6, the author is quoting from Ps. 40:6, where it clearly means sin offering, and in verse 8 he is writing on his own. We would suggest that the term "sin offering" occurred in the purpose clause of the pre-Pauline sending formula that Paul is using at Rom. 8:3–4. It would have read something like this: "God sent his Son in order that he might be a sin offering." Like another pre-Pauline formula in Rom. 3:25, "whom God put forward as an expiation [or, "means of atonement"; Greek: *hilastērion*]," this formula will come from those circles in Hellenistic Christianity that interpreted the death of Jesus in terms of the ceremonies of the Day of Atonement (*Yom Kippur*).[3] Paul's redactional expansions result in a further understanding of the soteriological purpose of the sending of the Son. Its effects are not only objective (sin offering) but subjective: "in order that the just requirement of the law might be fulfilled in us, who walk not according to the flesh but according to the Spirit." More important for our present purpose is the insertion of an explicit reference to the incarnation in the phrase "in the likeness of sinful flesh." This recalls a similar phrase in the pre-Pauline formula in Phil. 2:7, "being born in the likeness of men." It makes the reference to the incarnation unmistakable, and the sending will refer beyond all doubt to the sending of the preexistent One into the world at the moment of his birth. This clinches the interpretation of the Philippians hymn as a three-step Christology.

Wisdom and Preexistence

The Corinthian correspondence contains further relevant material for a preexistence/incarnation Christology in Paul. The Corinthians were going to excess in their enthusiasm for wisdom and knowledge (*gnosis*). Paul counteracts these tendencies by insisting that it is Christ crucified who embodies the wisdom of God:

> . . . we preach Christ crucified, a stumbling block to Jews and folly to Gentiles, but to those who are called, both Jews and Gentiles, Christ the power of God and the wisdom of God. (1 Cor. 1:23–24)

Paul's point is that Christians experience the wisdom of God not as a vague sort of revelation but concretely manifested in a particular history, a history that culminated in a physical death upon a cross. It would be an exaggeration, however, to construe this passage in terms of a full-blown wisdom Christology, as though Christ were the incarnation of preexistent Wisdom. Rather, Paul is speaking of Christ as he was present in the kerygma. In the preaching of the cross there is a revelation of the wisdom of God.

A few verses later, Paul again identifies Christ as the wisdom of God: " . . . Christ Jesus, whom God made our wisdom, our righteousness, sanctification and redemption" (1 Cor. 1:30). At first sight it looks as though wisdom was merely the first of a series of predicates that define the effects of Christ's work in the believers. But note that wisdom is separated from the other predicates by its own possessive pronoun ("our") and that it is distinguished from the other predicates by the absence of a copula ("and"). This means that wisdom is prior to the other three predicates: Christ is first and foremost our wisdom, and, as such, he effects in us righteousness, sanctification, and redemption. This leads us to ask when or at what point God made him our wisdom. Is Paul thinking here in terms of preexistent Wisdom becoming incarnate at Jesus' birth, as in a three-step Christology? Or was Jesus made the wisdom of God for us at the inauguration of his earthly ministry? Or did God make him his wisdom at his resurrection and exaltation? Probably Paul is again thinking of the kerygma, the preaching that began after Christ's death and resurrection. This is shown by the context. Paul had just said that it was through "the folly of what we preach" (literally, the folly of kerygma) that God chose to save the believers. Here we have the answer to our question: God made Jesus his saving wisdom when the kerygma began. And it was the kerygma that effected our righteousness, sanctification, and redemption. While Christ and wisdom here are identified in a functional sense, there is no thought in this passage that Christ is the incarnation of the preexistent Wisdom of God.

Later on in the same letter, Paul does identify Christ in his preexistence with the divine Wisdom. In 1 Cor. 8:6 we read the following:

For us there is one God, the Father,

41

> from whom are all things,
> and for whom we exist,
> and one Lord, Jesus Christ,
> through whom are all things,
> and through whom we exist.

True, there is no explicit mention of Wisdom here. But the activities ascribed to the pre-existent Christ are precisely the activities of Wisdom. He was the agent of creation, both of the universe in its entirety and of humanity in particular. Paul is drawing here upon a Wisdom tradition that goes back to the Book of Proverbs, where Wisdom says of herself,

> The Lord created me at the
> beginning of his work.
>
> . . . .
>
> When he established the heavens,
> I was there,
>
> . . . .
>
> when he marked out the foundations
> of the earth,
> then I was beside him like a master
> workman. (Prov. 8:22–30)

If "master workman" is the correct reading in the final verse just quoted, this will mean that, already in Proverbs, Wisdom is the actual agent of creation. However, there is another reading given in the RSV margin, namely, "little child." This would mean that Wisdom was like a child in her father's workshop, watching her father as he produces his artifacts. Probably this is the meaning here. Wisdom is as yet only associated with the activity of creation; she is not yet its agent.

In the Apocrypha, Wisdom is clearly recognized as the agent of creation. She is the "fashioner [Greek: *technitis*] of all things" (Wisd. of Sol. 7:22). This is the tradition Paul is drawing upon when he speaks of Christ as the agent of creation. It is odd that Paul does not specifically equate him with Wisdom as he did in the context of the kerygma. (To call attention to this distinction, we put *wisdom* in lower case when referring to the identification of Christ with wisdom in the kerygma but with a capital W for *Wisdom* when speaking of the implicit identification of Christ with Wisdom as the agent of creation.)

Preexistence is again implied in an allusive reference to the revelatory activity of Wisdom in 1 Cor. 10:4. Paul is here reminding his readers of certain events in the Exodus story that prefigure the Christian sacraments of baptism and Holy Communion. He writes as follows:

> Our fathers . . . all ate the same supernatural [or "spiritual" RSV margin] food and all drank the same supernatural drink. For they all drank from the supernatural Rock which followed them, and the Rock was Christ. (1 Cor. 10:3–4)

This identification of the Rock with Christ looks like another far-fetched rabbinical exegesis on the part of Paul. It was, however, suggested by the Jewish sapiential tradition where Wisdom was seen as active throughout Israel's sacred history. See, for instance, the Wisdom of Solomon, chapters 10 and 11. More particularly, the Hellenistic-Jewish philosopher-theologian Philo of Alexandria equates the Rock in the

Exodus story with Wisdom: "the flinty rock is the wisdom of God, from which he satisfies the thirsty souls that love God."[4] Both Philo and Paul seem to be drawing independently upon a Hellenistic-Jewish exegesis of the Exodus narrative. Unlike Philo, however, Paul does not specifically mention the divine Wisdom, but Wisdom is the implied middle term in his equation of Christ with the Rock: Christ=(Wisdom)=the Rock.

Finally, there is a passage in 2 Corinthians where Paul is trying to persuade the congregation to resume their collection for the saints at Jerusalem after they had abandoned it during the recent crisis. Paul marshals every conceivable argument for Christian stewardship, among them an argument based on the incarnation:

> You know the grace of our Lord Jesus Christ, that though he was rich, yet for your sake he became poor, so that by his poverty you might become rich. (2 Cor. 8:9)

Paul is writing here in his own words, but its drift is strikingly reminiscent of the pre-Pauline hymn in Phil. 2:6–11. The incarnation is here portrayed as the self-emptying of the preexistent One. In the pre-Pauline hymn, the preexistent Christ was described as being "in the form of God and enjoying equality with God." Here he is described as being rich. In Philippians, he assumed human likeness and took the form of a slave. Here he becomes poor. Again, as in the sending formula, the incarnation has a soteriological purpose, defined here in the terms of an exchange: that we through his poverty might become rich. It would be tempting to suppose that Paul has in mind the actual circumstances of Christ's birth as related in the infancy stories in Luke. But it is more likely that Paul is reflecting on the conditions of Jesus' earthly ministry: "the Son of man has nowhere to lay his head." Yet we may have here another glimpse into the workshop in which the birth stories were shaped.

Conclusion

Paul offers no systematic doctrine of Christ's preexistence and incarnation. Nor do the titles Paul uses to refer to the incarnation of the preexistent One show any consistency. The formulae that identify Jesus as the Son of God sent into the world presume that heaven was the point of departure for his mission, but they say nothing about his preexistent state or activity. The passages that do speak about the preexistent state and/or of the functions of the preexistent One, draw heavily upon the Wisdom tradition. The preexistent One enjoys equality with God. He is the agent of revelation and redemption in Israel's sacred history. But in none of these passages is he ever explicitly called the Wisdom of God or even the Son but only "Jesus Christ." Moreover, 1 Cor. 8:6 does not speak of the incarnation, though it is implied by the human name *Jesus*. Only on three occasions (Gal. 4:4; Phil. 2:7; and Rom. 1:3) is the birth of Jesus explicitly mentioned. In other passages it is only implied when Paul speaks of Christ's assumption of human flesh, with its weakness, liability to sin, subjection to the law, and mortality. Paul equates Jesus with wisdom only when speaking of his presence in the kerygma. The apostle is never interested in preexistence, incarnation, or Jesus' birth for their own sake but only when he wants to make a point about their soteriological purpose or when enunciating an ethical demand (see Phil. 2:5 and 2 Cor. 8:8). There are a lot of loose ends in Paul's doctrine of the incarnation and in his view of the birth of Jesus as a significant christological moment. Those loose ends will only be tied up later, in the New Testament and in the development of doctrine in the later church.

At the same time, however, Paul offers us a few glimpses of the raw materials out of which the birth stories will later be constructed: Christ's Davidic descent (which Paul preserved from earlier tradition); the divine initiative in the sending of the Son; the role of the Holy Spirit in the conception/birth of significant figures in sacred history; and perhaps also the circumstance of poverty into which the Son of God was born.

Excursus: The Origin of Incarnational Christology

If our exegesis of the pre-Pauline hymn in Phil. 2:6–11 is correct, Paul did not invent the three-step Christology, with its portrait of Christ as a preexistent divine reality who assumed human flesh at birth. Rather, Paul took over this pattern of Christology from those circles who first composed the hymn. This pattern was independently adopted in other circles, by the author of the Letter to the Hebrews, as well as by the authors of the Johannine writings. It is a reasonable conjecture that the three-step Christology originated in the same Hellenistic-Jewish Christian circles that developed the atonement theology first found in another pre-Pauline formula, namely, Rom.3:25.[5] But where did these circles derive their incarnational Christology?

One popular view, first proposed by the History of Religions school in Germany during the earlier part of this century and continued by Rudolf Bultmann and his pupils until the sixties, was that it was derived from the pre-Christian, Gnostic redeemer myth, sometimes called the myth of the "redeemed redeemer." Allegedly, this myth originated in Iran some centuries previously.

In 1961 there appeared in Germany a work that conclusively demonstrated that the pre-Christian Gnostic redeemer myth was a figment of the critical imagination, an artificial construct of the History of Religions school.[6] But some scholars still look for the origins of the incarnational Christology in some non-Christian mythology.

In the controversy about the "myth of God incarnate," which took place in Britain during the 1970s, Michael Goulder proposed a theory that the early Christians borrowed the pattern of preexistence/incarnation from a Samaritan myth. Goulder admits that there is no direct evidence about Samaritan religious thinking in the first century C.E. He has to reconstruct it from later sources and in part from the New Testament (NT) itself. The idea of a preexistent entity in the Godhead, he suggests, is found in a fourth-century Samaritan document called

"The Teaching of Marqar." The Samaritans accepted only the Pentateuch, and they believed that there had been no revelation of saving activity of God since Moses. God had revealed himself to Moses in a series of abstractions, as Power, Truth, Wisdom, and Eternal Life. These abstractions were conceived as a kind of second person of a *Binity* similar to the later Christian doctrine of the Trinity. This, of course, says nothing about the incarnation of the second person. For that, Goulder turns to the story of Simon Magus in Acts 8:9–13. There we read of Simon Magus appearing in Samaria and claiming to be "somebody great." The Samaritans welcomed him and recognized him as "that power of God which is called Great." Putting these two pieces of evidence together, Goulder deduces that Simon Magus was, in his own estimate and that of the Samaritans, the incarnation of the second person of the Samaritan Binity. To the present writer, however, Goulder seems to read more into the Marqar document than it can bear. There is no real suggestion in the document that the Power, Truth, and Wisdom of God constituted a kind of second person within the deity. Rather, it looks like a Samaritan variant of the general speculation on Wisdom that was current in Judaism at the time. Again, Goulder's combination of evidence from the fourth century with that of the first (Marqar and Simon Magus) is questionable. More than that, Acts hardly presents Simon Magus as an incarnation of the second person of the Godhead. He was probably no more than a Hellenistic miracle worker, a divine man (*theios anēr*), i.e., an epiphany rather than an incarnation of the deity. Nor is it clear that Simon had anything to do with Samaritan theology. This is especially unlikely if, in that theology, divine revelation ceased with Moses and the Pentateuch. At the same time we should recognize an element of truth in Goulder's theory. The picture of Moses as the revealer of the divine Wisdom may provide useful evidence for the type of Judaism the author of John's Gospel is combating (see chap. 6).

A different mythical origin for the incarnational Christology of early Christianity has been proposed more recently by Harold Attridge.[7] He believes there was an ancient and widespread myth of a divine hero who descended from heaven into the underworld to rescue the dead and restore them to life. Earlier forms of this myth are found in the stories of Orpheus and Herakles. This mythic pattern, according to Attridge, found its way in various adaptations into Greco-Roman, Jewish, Christian, and Gnostic myths of redemption.

As an explanation of the origin of the early church's incarnational Christology, this suggestion is too vague to be convincing. It may, however, explain how the incarnational Christology eventually won out in gentile Christianity and supplanted all the other christological patterns, such as the two-step Christology and the historical-sending formula.

The incarnational Christology is better seen as an internal development within early Christianity. It is the result of the combining of earlier christological patterns with the wisdom Christology. This can be seen clearly in the pre-Pauline Philippians hymn. The second part of the hymn clearly represents a two-step Christology. After his death, Jesus was exalted and given the name of *Kyrios* (Lord). It is thus very similar to Rom. 1:4 and Acts 2:36. To this earlier two-step pattern, the pre-Pauline Hellenistic-Jewish community would have added the earlier part about the preexistent One who was in the form of God and his self-manifestation in human likeness. This combination results in a certain tension in the three-step pattern thus produced. If the preexistent One was already equal with God, how could he later acquire the divine name *Kyrios*, the name that is above all other names? The incarnational Christology requires no external influences, other than that of the Jewish wisdom speculation, to explain it. It is not the result of external borrowing. Scholars always seem reluctant to admit this. They suffer from what a Jewish NT scholar, Samuel Sandmel, called "parallelomania."

5. Incarnational Christology after Paul

Colossians

The Epistle to the Colossians is one of those letters whose Pauline authorship is in question—less perhaps than Ephesians and less still than the Pastorals. The best solution of the problem of Colossians is to assume that it was written by a disciple of Paul toward the end of the apostle's lifetime and under his authority. This would explain the differences of style, vocabulary, and, to some extent, of thought, though that is due in part to the language used by the Colossian "heretics." At the time Colossians was written, Paul was in prison (Col. 4:3, 10, 18), probably in Rome. The apostle must have read the letter, adding a postscript in his "own hand" (4:18).

Colossians deals with a rather different situation from those of the letters Paul wrote himself. The community being addressed is tempted to succumb to a "philosophy" (Col. 2:8). This is not a respectable philosophy like those of Plato, Aristotle, or the Stoics but the kind of theosophy in which "thrones, dominions, principalities, and authorities" (Col. 1:16) were worshiped as angelic powers (Col. 2:18). This can hardly mean that the Colossians were abandoning their belief in Christ. Rather, they thought that the revelation of the gospel was incomplete and needed to be supplemented by further revelations from the angelic powers.

In combating this "heresy," the author insists on the finality of Christ, both in creation and redemption. In doing this, the author draws upon a Wisdom hymn similar to the formula Paul himself had used in 1 Cor. 8:6 (see above, pp. 41-42). It reads as follows:

> He[1] is the image of the invisible God,
> the first-born of all creation;
> for in him all things were created,
> in heaven and on earth.
> . . . .
> He is before all things,
> and in him all things hold together.
> He is the head of the body.
> (Col. 1:15–16a, 17–18a)

The subject of this hymn is designated in verse 13 as "his [God's] beloved Son." Thus the author identifies the preexistent One as the Son of God just as Paul had done in his redaction of the sending formula (see above, pp. 37-38). But he goes beyond Paul in explicitly identifying the preexistent Son of God as One who fulfills the functions of divine Wisdom. The Colossians hymn also goes beyond what Paul had said in 1 Cor. 8:6 in attributing to the preexistent One the further function of upholding the universe: "in him all things hold together" (v. 17). In order to relate this hymn to the situation at Colossae, the author redacts the hymn, adding that "all things" include "thrones, dominions, principalities, and authorities." These powers were inferior to the preexistent One because they owe their creation to him. In the original hymn, the phrase "he is the head of the body" apparently referred to the universe or cosmos, which in Stoicism was identified as a body. But in his redaction of the hymn, the author glosses the word *body* as the church, thus picking up an image Paul himself had developed in 1 Cor. 12:12–27 and Rom. 12:4–5. In this way the author prepares to extend the hymn to cover not only creation but redemption. So he adds another stanza to the hymn (whether this is in prose or in verse is disputed). The addition reads as follows:

> . . . he is the beginning, the first-born from the dead, that in everything he might be pre-eminent. For in him all the fulness of God was pleased to dwell, and through him to reconcile to himself all things, whether on earth or in heaven, making peace by the blood of his cross.
> (Col. 1:18c–20)

Once again "all things" will include the powers. Thus, Christ is superior to them, not only in creation, but also in redemption. By reconciling them, he has asserted his lordship over them as in the final stanza of the Philippians hymn.

The author does not explicitly state that the preexistent One became incarnate in a human birth, but this is obviously implied in the reference to the "blood of his cross." This implication is clinched a few lines later when we read that the reconciliation took place "in his body of flesh by his death" (v. 22). And although the author does not say so, it would have been at birth that the preexistent One assumed the body of his flesh. It was in this incarnate state that he triumphed over the very powers that at Colossae threatened to undermine the uniqueness of Christ. The Colossians had forgotten that Christ had triumphed over the powers:

> He disarmed the principalities and powers and made a public example of them, triumphing over them in it. (RSV margin; sc., the cross, Col. 2:15)

There is one other possible reference to the incarnation in Colossians. This is in 2:9, where we read the following: "For in him the whole fulness of deity dwells bodily [Greek: *sōmatikōs*]." Does "bodily" refer to the body of incarnation? The present tense of the word *dwells* suggests rather that the author is speaking of Christ's resurrection body. If so, the word *fulness* is used in the same post-resurrection context as in 2:10, which speaks of what happened after Christ became the first-born of the dead. The author of Colossians wants to assure his readers that the "fulness" of redemption is present in the risen Christ and they need not, therefore, hanker after the angelic powers, or "elemental spirits" as he calls them in 2:8.

Ephesians

The Epistle to the Ephesians is more likely to be a deutero-Pauline letter than Colossians. It was almost certainly written after the apostle's death and is a rewriting of Colossians to adapt it to a quite different situation. This situation is difficult to determine with precision, but it clearly has to do with the unity of Jew and Gentile in the one Church as the Body of Christ. It seems to have been written to gentile Christians who were in danger of forgetting the Jewish origins of their faith and of abandoning their Jewish heritage.[2] The author reminds his readers that on the cross Christ has destroyed the barrier between Jew and Gentile. In Colossians, it was the powers that were reconciled by the cross; in Ephesians, it is Jew and Gentile. In making his point, our author takes up a passage in Colossians and introduces an emphasis on the incarnation that was not explicit in the original. We set the two passages in parallel columns so the reader can see what has happened:

Col. 2:14	*Eph. 2:14–15*
	For he is our peace; who has made us both one, and broken down the dividing wall of hostility
having canceled the bond which stood against us with its legal demands; this he set aside, nailing it to the cross.	by abolishing *in his flesh* the law of commandments and ordinances, that he might create in himself one new man in place of the two, so making peace.

The author of Ephesians has dropped the metaphor of nailing the "bond" to the cross since it was less relevant for his purpose and has substituted another metaphor, that of the wall that divided Jew and Gentile, as in the Temple in Jerusalem. The phrase we have italicized, "in his flesh," denotes here the physical body of Christ offered as a sacrifice on the cross.

Does this mean that the author of Ephesians held a Christology of preexistence and incarnation? Another passage may serve as proof that Ephesians did hold to a three-step Christology. In Eph. 4:9–10, he is commenting on the word *ascended* in Ps. 68:18, which he has just quoted:

> In saying "he ascended," what does he mean but that he also descended to the lower parts of the earth. "He that descended is the same who ascended . . ."

Does "lower parts of the earth" mean the underworld or earth as opposed to heaven? In the former case, the author would be referring to Christ's descent to Hades after death. In the latter, it would mean the incarnation, the first occurrence of "descend" in that connection.

The Pastorals

Like the other pastoral Epistles, 2 Timothy is written to encourage the believers of a postapostolic generation to remain faithful to the tradition that had been handed down to them from Paul. Several quotations from creedlike formulae summarize the teaching of Paul. One of them, in 2 Tim. 2:8, reads as follows:

> Remember Jesus Christ, risen from the dead, descended from David as preached in my [sc., Paul's] gospel.

This is a curious summary of Paul's gospel. Not only does the Davidic descent (literally, "of the seed of David") come after the mention of the resurrection, it is hardly a true representation of

Paul's distinctive gospel. As we saw, Paul only twice referred to Jesus' Davidic descent (Rom. 1:3; 15:12). All we can say is that the author of 2 Timothy considered Jesus' birth as a descendent of David, "the root of Jesse," to be of some christological importance.

There are two hymnic fragments in 1 Timothy that have a bearing on the subject of Christ's incarnation. One occurs in 2:5–6 and reads as follows:

> . . . there is one God,
> and there is one mediator
> between God and men,
> the man Christ Jesus,
> who gave himself as a ransom for all,
> the testimony to which was borne at the
> proper time.

This fragment does not speak of the pre-existence of Christ but only of his existence as a man, giving himself up as a ransom for all. Christ stands in the middle between God and humanity, sharing by implication the nature of both. He accomplishes the divine work of the redemption in humanity and for humanity. Since there is nothing here about preexistence, we cannot be sure that the idea of incarnation is implied. It is interesting that some commentators who accept the idea of a redeemer myth (see chap. 4) think that this myth lies behind this hymn. In that case, the hymn would indeed presuppose an incarnational Christology and, therefore, a human birth.

The latter possibility becomes more likely in another hymn or fragment of a hymn in the same Epistle. This reads as follows:

A   He was manifested in the flesh,
B   vindicated in the Spirit,
B   seen by angels,
A   preached among the nations,
A   believed on in the world,
B   taken up in glory. (1 Tim. 3:16)

This hymn operates at two levels: an earthly level and a heavenly. We have designated the lines that refer to the earthly level by an *A* and those that refer to a heavenly level by a *B*. This produces a chiastic form: *A-B, B-A, A-B*.[3] The reader will notice the absence of an initial *B*, indicating that the hymn does not start with reference to Christ's preexistence. But that is surely implied in the word *manifested*. That which was manifested was previously hidden; that which was disclosed in the flesh previously existed outside of the flesh. Thus, 1 Tim. 3:16 is a statement of the incarnation: "The beginning of the hymn assumes as self-evident that Christ belongs to the heavenly world of God."[4]

Hebrews: An Appendix to the Pauline Corpus

In the canon of Scripture, Hebrews appears as an appendix to the Pauline corpus. The other letters of the corpus are arranged according to length, Romans being the longest and Philemon the shortest. Hebrews is a long letter, but it is placed after Philemon. It is an anonymous writing of the second generation after the apostles. However, as Heb. 13:23, with its reference to Timothy, indicates, the author had some connection with the Pauline circle. Hebrews has a distinct theology of its own, but it draws on the same traditions of Hellenistic-

Jewish Christianity (probably emanating from the Stephen circle) as did Paul. Like Paul, the Christology of Hebrews combines both the two-step and the three-step type. The two-step Christology is reflected in the use of such texts as Ps. 2:7 and Ps. 110:1 (see chap. 2). The writing begins with a formula, perhaps of a hymnic kind, that clearly expresses a three-step Christology:

> . . . through whom he created the world.
> He [Greek: who] reflects the glory of God
> and bears the very stamp of his nature,
> upholding the universe by his word
>   of power.
> When he had made purification for sins,
> he sat down at the right hand of the
>   Majesty on high,
> having become as much superior to
>   the angels
> as the name he has obtained is more
>   excellent than theirs.
>
> (Heb. 1:2c–4)

There are several interesting features about this hymn, which become apparent when we compare it with the christological hymns we have looked at thus far. Like the Colossians hymn, it begins with a reference to the relationship of the preexistent One to God, to his agency in his creation, and to his upholding of the universe. Moreover, like the Colossians hymn as it now stands, it moves straight from the first step to the third, from preexistence to exaltation, though implying by its allusion to the atonement the second step, the incarnation.

That the author did have the incarnation in

his mind is shown by the catena of eight OT citations, all of which (except one that refers to the angels) are christological in import and serve to buttress the hymn with which the letter began.

Generations of Anglicans, including Episcopalians in the United States, have heard Heb. 1:1–12, and therefore most of the catena of citations, as the Epistle for Christmas Day. Since 1979, however, it has been relegated to the third eucharist of the day, where it is least likely to be heard. As they listened to it on Christmas Day, most worshipers probably connected the first two citations with the birth of Christ:

> "Thou art my Son,
> today I have begotten thee."
>
> . . . .
>
> "I will be to him a father,
> and he shall be to me a son."

The first of these two texts, Ps. 2:7, was applied in early Christianity to the enthronement of Christ at his exaltation, as we saw when discussing the pre-Pauline formula in Rom. 1:3–4. In the course of time, its application was shifted backward and, in combination with Isa. 42:1, became the voice from heaven at Jesus' baptism:

> "Thou art my beloved Son; with thee I am
> well pleased. " (Mark 1:11)

It has recently been argued that Hebrews has shifted the application of Ps. 2:7 even further back, to the eternal generation of the pre-existent Son. The same shift will have taken place in the second text, 2 Sam. 7:14, which, it is alleged, refers to the eternal relation of the Father and the Son.[5] This construal is based on the assumption that our catena follows an orderly pattern from preexistence through incarnation and birth to exaltation. Unfortunately, however, the citations do not follow the orderly pattern, for the seventh one, from Ps. 102:25–27, cited in Heb. 1:10–12, clearly refers to the Son's agency in creating the world:

> "Thou, Lord, didst found the earth
> in the beginning,
> and the heavens are the work of thy
> hands . . . "

The quotation continues to speak of the eternity of the Son:

> " . . . But thou art the same,
> and thy years will never end."

Thus, the seventh text embraces a preexistent and exalted state. It is, therefore, difficult to discern a coherent christological pattern in the catena. The reason is that all the way through our author is interested, not in the Christology for its own sake, but in the superiority of the Son over the angels. This is shown by the introduction to the catena: "For to what angel did God ever say . . .?" This introduction covers the two following quotations, as the word *again,* which introduces each of them, shows. Also, this explains why the fourth quotation is not about Christology but about the angels:

> Of the angels he says,
>   "Who makes his angels winds,
>   and his servants flames of fire."
> (Heb. 1:7)

One quotation, however, quite clearly refers to the birth of the eternal Son. This is the third one:

> And again, when he brings the first-born into
> the world,
> he says,
> "Let all God's angels worship him."
> (Heb. 1:6)

Here we have for the first time in Hebrews an unmistakable allusion to the birth of Christ. It even looks like a direct reference to the Christmas story. In Luke, however, the angels did not worship the Christ child. There, one angel announces the birth, and a chorus of angels sings the Gloria in Excelsis, so the parallel is not exact. All the same, we may have here another glimpse into the workshop in which the birth narratives were constructed. At any rate, Hebrews and Luke agree that in one way or another the angels played a role in the birth of Christ. Another interesting feature of the introduction to the quotation is the description of Christ as the "first-born." This echoes another messianic testimony, Ps. 89:27, which reads as follows:

> I will make him the first-born,
> the highest of the kings of the earth.

This text also was originally applied in early Christianity to the exaltation of Christ, as in Rom. 8:29.

Curiously, the catena includes no citations about the work of the incarnate Son on earth, nothing, e.g., to support the statement in the formula about the "purification for sins" (Heb.

1:3). This omission is probably explained by the fact that the rest of Hebrews will expound at great length the atoning work of Christ and the inauguration of the new covenant through his death.

In expounding the significance of Christ's death and exaltation, interpreted in terms of high priesthood, the author attaches considerable importance to the incarnation and the humanity of Christ. But as in Paul, they are important for the end rather than for the beginning of Christ's earthly life.

Thus, the author of Hebrews insists that our great high priest had to "share in flesh and blood" (the Greek actually reads "blood and flesh," doubtless because for our author blood is especially important in connection with the atonement). The author sets out no less than five reasons for the incarnation: It was necessary (1) for the destruction of the devil; (2) to deliver humanity from the fear of death; (3) because the beneficiaries were not angels but the "descendants of Abraham" (cf. Paul's discussion of the seed of Abraham and see above, chap.4); (4) because, as one who was like us in every respect, he could make "expiation" for sins; and (5) as our great high priest in heaven, he could help us when we are tempted, having known temptation himself. The last of these points is developed further a little later:

> For we have not a high priest who is unable to sympathize with our weaknesses, but one who in every respect has been tempted as we are, yet without sin. (Heb. 4:15)

Had he not become incarnate in a human birth, he could have not have been subject to temptation. But because of that, we can find in our exalted high priest "grace to help in time of need" (Heb. 4:16). This is a unique exposition of the religious value of the incarnation. It extends, not only to the cross, but also to the continuing work of Christ in his exalted state. Thus, the incarnation is doubly important for the cross and for the heavenly intercession.

A little later we read,

> In the days of his flesh, Jesus offered up prayers and supplications with loud cries and tears to him who was able to save him from death. (Heb. 5:7)

This looks like a reference to Gethsemane, though that is disputed. But in any case, the stress on the incarnation is evident in the words "in the days of his flesh."

In a remarkable exposition of the Septuagint version of Ps. 40:6–8, our author exploits the peculiarity of the Greek translation:

> Consequently, when Christ came into the
>   world, he said,
>   "Sacrifices and offerings thou hast not
>   desired,
>   but a body hast thou prepared for me;
>   in burnt offerings and sin offerings thou
>   hast taken no pleasure.
>   Then I said, 'Lo, I have come to do thy
>   will, O God,'
>   as it is written of me in the role of the
>   book."
>
> (Heb. 10:5–7)

As any commentary will show, the Hebrew reads, "but my ears you have pierced," rather than, "a body thou hast prepared for me." The psalmist was protesting against the substitution of cultic sacrifice for ethical obedience. The Septuagint's translation enables our author to give a christological twist to the text and, in doing so, to refer explicitly to the birth of Christ ("when Christ came into the world") as the moment of the incarnation. At that point, the preexistent One assumed a body he could offer as a sacrifice of perfect obedience to achieve atonement on the cross of Calvary.

Like Paul, the author of Hebrews values the beginning of Jesus' mission, his incarnation and birth, not for its own sake but because it was the essential preliminary to the salvation that was accomplished on the cross. The difference between them is that they conceive that salvation differently. For Paul, the incarnation meant submission to the law in order to redeem those who are under the law. For Hebrews, the incarnation meant sharing in the weakness, temptation, and mortality of humankind in order that they might be saved from sin and death and have a high priest in heaven who could sympathize with their infirmities and grant them grace to help in time of need.

6. The Johannine Writings

In chapter 1 we noted that the synoptic Gospels enshrine three stages of tradition: the authentic sayings of Jesus and authentic memories of his deeds; the shaping of these materials in the oral tradition of the post-Easter community; and the interpretation of these traditions in the redactions of the Evangelists. With the Gospel of John, the situation is more complicated. The memories of Jesus' words and works and of his career culminating in death all claim to rest on the witness of the Beloved Disciple (John 21:24). They represent a tradition that at some points (viz., the beginning of Jesus' ministry, the central crisis, and its ending with the Passion and Easter events) coincides, broadly speaking, with the synoptic tradition. At these points, the Gospel of John can be used to substantiate, to supplement, and even to correct the synoptists. Other materials, such as the distinctive Johannine signs, are peculiar to the Johannine tradition. It is impossible to know to what extent these traditions go back to the Beloved Disciple, but at some stage they were combined into a continuous Gospel, usually called the *Signs Gospel*, though *Narrative Gospel* might be a more accurate designation since it consists of other narratives besides miracle stories. Concurrently, the sayings of Jesus circulating in the Johannine community were being developed into continuous discourses. The Narrative Gospel was later expanded by the addition of the discourse material. This was the work of the Johannine writer whom we call the Evangelist, and we will call it the *Discourse Gospel*.

Until recently, the Johannine community had existed within the Jewish community and had worshiped in the synagogue. Now the Johannine community has been expelled from the synagogue (John 9:22; cf. 12:42; 16:2). The Evangelist seeks to boost the morale of the Johannine Christians by reassuring them that Jesus Christ is the definitive revelation of God, not Moses, as the synagogue claimed. Evidently, the type of Judaism the Evangelist was combating was the same as we met earlier in our discussion of Samaritan theology (see chap. 4). After its expulsion from the synagogue, the Johannine community attracted to itself gentile converts who understood the Discourse Gospel in a docetic-gnostic sense. Jesus brought to the world light, life, and truth, but the revelation he brought could be detached from his person. His humanity was a matter of indifference. Tensions within the community led these docetic-gnostics to withdraw and set up a community of their own. All this is described in the first Epistle of John. There we read that the docetic-gnostics were identified as the Antichrist (1 John 2:18). "They went out from us, but they were not of us" (1 John 2:19). They denied that Jesus had "come in the flesh" (1 John 4:2; cf. 2 John 7). In response to this situation, another member of the Johannine community, whom we call the Redactor, made certain additions to the Discourse Gospel to rule out the docetic-gnostic interpretation. The Redactor prefaced the Gospel with a prologue (John 1:1–18). He spliced this prologue into the original beginning of this Gospel (John 1:6–8, 15, and continuing with vv. 19 ff.). The prologue reached its climax in the statement that in Jesus the Word became "flesh"—a term the docetists would have abhorred. Similarly, in John 6:51–58, the author adds to the bread discourse a section about eating the flesh and drinking the blood of the Son of man, an idea that would have been even more abhorrent to the docetists.

"Low" Christology in John

Traditionally, John's Gospel has been interpreted throughout as the expression of a "high" Christology of preexistence and incarnation. Thus, when the Johannine Jesus speaks of his being "sent," of his "coming," or of his "being from above," this has been understood as a sending or coming from heaven at birth. Taken by themselves, however, such expressions need be no more than the historical sending or coming of a prophet.[1] Similar expressions occur in the synoptic tradition, which knows nothing of a preexistence/incarnation Christology. Thus, in the synoptic tradition, Jesus can speak of himself as the Son of man who "*came* eating and drinking" (Matt. 11:18 par. Q) just as the Baptist came neither eating nor drinking. Similarly, in Mark, Jesus says that he "came not to call the righteous, but sinners" (Mark 2:17).

69

Many of the Johannine statements about the coming or sending of Jesus could be read in this way. Take, for instance, John 5:43. Here the Johannine Christ says,

> I have come in my Father's name, and you
> do not receive me;
> If another comes in his own name, him
> you will receive.

The parallelism between Jesus and the "others" shows that in each case the coming is a purely historical mission. There are two Greek words for "sending" (*pempō* and *apostellō*); both verbs are used in contexts that refer unmistakably to historical sending. Thus, in John 4:34, the Johannine Jesus says, "My food is to do the will of him who sent (Greek: *pempsantos*) me," and in 17:18 he places his own mission and his sending of the disciples in parallelism, showing that both are historical missions:

> As thou didst send [Greek: *apesteilas*] me
> into the world,
> so I have sent [Greek: *apesteila*] them
> into the world,

This last quotation is particularly instructive because it shows that "into the world" does not necessarily refer to preexistence and incarnation in respect to Jesus any more than it does in the case of the disciples. His mission, like theirs, was historical.

What about those passages where Jesus speaks of himself as being "from God"? Even such sayings do not necessarily require an incarnational interpretation. Take for instance this saying:

> Not that anyone has seen the Father
> except him who is from [Greek: *para*] God;
> he has seen the Father. (John 6:46)

This seeing of the Father need not refer, at least in the earlier stages of the Johannine tradition, to the eternal relation of the preexistent One to his Father but rather to the Abba experience of the historical Jesus (see below).

The earlier Johannine tradition also contained sayings in which Jesus is evidently the spokesperson of Wisdom. It is easy to imagine that some of the great "I am" sayings were originally spoken by the Johannine Jesus as sayings of Wisdom. Thus, the saying in John 6:35–37 may well have read originally as follows:

> The Wisdom of God says, "I am the bread
>   of life;
> he who comes to me shall not hunger;
> and he who comes to me I will not cast
>   out."

The situation here would be similar to that of the Savior's appeal in Matt. 11:28–30 (see above, pp. 28-29). Like that saying, the bread of heaven saying could be very early tradition, even if not an authentic saying of the earthly Jesus. In that case, the history of the tradition of this saying would be similar to that of the Q saying in Matt. 23:34–35 (see above, pp. 29-30).

"High" Christology

In response to the situation created by the expulsion of the Johannine community from the synagogue, the Evangelist developed a much

71

higher Christology. The Johannine Jesus became not merely the spokesperson of Wisdom but personally identical with that figure. The introductory "Wisdom says" was dropped. With this resultant heightened Christology, the Jesus of the Evangelist came to speak of his own preexistence and descent from heaven. This is clear from the preamble to the foot-washing:

> Jesus, knowing that the Father had given all things into his hands, and that he had come from God and was going to God. . . . (John 13:3)

In a similar vein, Jesus affirms his preexistence in the exordium of the high priestly prayer:

> . . . and now, Father, glorify thou me in thy own presence with the glory which I had with thee before the world was made. (John 17:5)

Only One who was personally identical with Wisdom could make such a startling claim.[2] Jesus can, therefore, speak of himself in the Johannine discourses as the Son of man who came down from heaven and who will ascend to heaven again:

> No one has ascended into heaven but he who descended from heaven, the Son of man. (John 3:13)

Similarly, Jesus can say of himself:

> I have come down from heaven, not to do my own will, but the will of him who sent me. (John 6:38)

This language of descent and of coming down from heaven can not mean simply a prior mystical experience of the earthly Jesus, as John A. T. Robinson argues: "Heaven is where he belongs, his home; his life is in the realms above, 'hidden with God,' as Paul might have put it."[3] Coupled with the language of the high priestly prayer, the incarnational meaning of descent is inescapable.

By introducing this higher Christology into the discourses, the Evangelist opened up a reinterpretation of the earlier and lower Christology. The passages that spoke about Jesus as having come or being sent will now refer not merely to his historical mission but to the incarnation of the preexistent One. They thus acquire a double meaning, a meaning at two different levels, a technique characteristic of the Evangelist. We can see this happening in the phrase "him who sent me" in John 6:38, quoted above.

The eschatological prophet of the earlier discourse material has been transformed into a preexistent One who became incarnate on earth and was exalted into heaven. This, we saw, has been achieved through the transformation of Jesus into One who is personally identical with the divine Wisdom. It was the polemic against the Moses mysticism of the synagogue and its claim that Moses was the embodiment of the divine Wisdom. When Jesus says, "I am the bread of life" (John 6:35, etc.) the "I" is emphatic like Louis XIV's "*l'état c'est moi.*" The Evangelist thus did not develop this higher Christology as an academic exercise but in response to the claims of the synagogue about Moses and the Torah.

The question now arises, When was the moment of the incarnation? It would be natural to suppose that it was at the birth of Jesus or at his conception. This, after all, was the Christology of the Pauline corpus. The Discourse Gospel, however, has no birth narrative but, as we have seen, began like Mark with the ministry of the Baptist and inauguration of Jesus' earthly career. In the light of this, it would seem that the Evangelist has retained the christological perspective of the earlier Johannine tradition, which saw in the baptism of Jesus the supreme christological moment.[4] It was then that the preexistent Wisdom was sent from heaven and came into the world, then that it came from heaven. Two passages make this clear. The first is John 3:34.

> For he whom God has sent utters the words of God, for it is not by measure that he gives the Spirit.

In this passage, the sending of the Son is closely connected with the giving of the Spirit, and it was at this baptism that Jesus received a plenary endowment of the Spirit (see John 1:33). The second passage is John 6:27, which speaks of Jesus' baptismal sealing: ". . . for on him has God the Father set his seal" (viz., making him the bread from heaven).

Elsewhere, the Discourse Gospel adopts a surprisingly negative attitude towards Jesus' birth. In chapter 7, the Johannine Jesus engages in a controversy with the synagogue Jews, which reflects the conflict that was going on between the Johannine community and the synagogue of their own day:

When they heard these words, some of the people said, "This is really the prophet." Others said, "This is the Christ." But some said, "Is the Christ to come from Galilee? Has not the scripture said that the Christ is descended from David, and comes from Bethlehem, the village where David was?" (John 7:40–42)

A little later a similar objection is raised: "Search and you will see that no prophet is to rise from Galilee" (John 7:52). We have here an interesting glimpse into the kind of discussion that must have gone on about the birth of Jesus, perhaps among Christians themselves as well as between the Christians and the synagogue Jews. While Jesus' Davidic descent seems to have been accepted without question, there may well have been discussion about his place of birth, given the fact that he was known to have come from Nazareth. But how does this square with the prophecy of Mic. 5:2? This contains the following prediction:

But you, O Bethlehem Ephrathah,
 who are little to be among the
  clans of Judah,
from you shall come forth for me
 one who is to be ruler in Israel,
whose origin is from of old,
 from ancient days.

There appears to be no clear evidence that this passage was interpreted messianically in Judaism, and we have no means of knowing precisely at what point it was so interpreted in the early Church and applied to Jesus' birth (see below, p. 88, for its use at Matt. 2:6). While the Matthean community accepted the tradition of Jesus' birth at Bethlehem, the Johannine Evangelist took a different line. What mattered to him was not whether Jesus was of Davidic descent; the point was that Jesus was from heaven and was sent by God into the world:

> You know me, and you know where I come from? But I have not come of my own accord; he who sent me is true, and him you do not know. I know him, for I come from him, and he sent me. (John 7:28–29)

In a way, the Johannine attitude to the birth of Jesus was fraught with danger. It could easily lead to a docetic reading of the Discourse Gospel, as though Jesus came only from above and had no ordinary human birth. We shall see later how the Johannine Redactor had to face this problem.

In one further controversy the question of Jesus' birth comes indirectly to the fore. In the dialogue between Jesus and the synagogue Jews about their claim to be descended from Abraham, the Johannine Jesus accuses them of being untrue to their origin. Abraham had accepted the revelation of God now incarnate in Jesus. Therefore, they could not be Abraham's children (John 8:39). This leads them to protest: "We were not born of fornication" (v.41). In the Greek, the pronoun *we* is emphatic, as if to say, "*we* aren't illegitimate like you." Perhaps we have here indirect evidence that the tradition of Jesus' virginal conception was already current. There are two possibilities. Either the allegation of illegitimacy preceded the tradition of the virginal conception, or the accusation of illegitimacy was a riposte to that tradition. In either case, we have here yet another glimpse into the development of the birth narratives. Once again, however, the Johannine Evangelist adopts a neutral attitude. What matters is not whether Jesus was conceived out of wedlock or whether he was conceived of a virgin. What mattered was that he was sent by the Father and came from heaven.

Thus far the Evangelist's attitude to Jesus' birth is purely negative. There is, however, another dialogue in which the Johannine Jesus refers to his birth in more positive terms. In the trial before Pilate, the governor asks him about his alleged claim to be king of the Jews (John 18:33). As in the synoptic tradition, Jesus refuses to answer yes or no. Instead, he tries to define what kingship really means:

> My kingship is not of this world; if my kingship were of this world, my servants would fight, that I might not be handed over to the Jews; but my kingship is not from the world. (John 18:36)

Pilate takes this to be tantamount to the claim of kingship: "So you are a king, then?" This elicits from Jesus the solemn reply,

> You say that I am a king. For this was I born, and for this I have come into the world, to bear witness to the truth. (John 18:37)

Here at last is a direct reference to Jesus' birth, repeated in the phrase "I have come into the world." Moreover, the birth of Jesus is given a positive christological purpose. It was "to bear witness to the truth." This is a Johannine equivalent to saying, "to be the bearer of God's revelation." Note, however, that Jesus does not bear witness to the truth immediately upon birth. He requires a later commissioning in order to take up the purpose for which he was born. The birth of Jesus is only a *preliminary* christological moment. The more important moment remains the inauguration of his mission at his baptism. Only then does he begin to bear witness to the truth. Only then is he actively the Word made flesh. Only then do we see his glory. The incarnation in Johannine thought is not the combination of two substances, humanity and divinity, which took place at Jesus' birth. Rather, it is a dynamic relationship in which Jesus constantly responds in obedience to the Father.

This dynamic character of the incarnation is brought out in the way in which the Evangelist develops the theme of the Father/Son relationship. This, of course, has its roots in the Abba experience of the historical Jesus. But as in the case of the other earlier Christologies, Jesus as prophet and as the spokesperson of Wisdom, the Father/Son Christology is developed much further. Take, for instance, the submerged parable in John 5:19–20. In its original form it was a true parable that must have read something like this:

My relationship to God is like that which I had with my earthly father, a carpenter. A son can do nothing of his own accord but only what he sees his father doing. For whatever the father does, the son imitates. For any father loves his son and shows him all the works he does.

The Evangelist has christologized the original parable so that it becomes a statement of the relationship between Jesus as Son and God as his Father. In his constant communion with the Father, Jesus learns the words and works he must perform. His own words and works thus become the words and the works of the Father. Hence, Jesus can say that his food is "to do the will of him who sent me and to accomplish his work" (John 4:34). The works are the works that "the Father has granted me to accomplish" (John 5:36). Through that communion, Jesus dwells in the Father and the Father in him (see John 14:11). This is what makes Jesus the One who bears witness to the truth, the Revealer of God, the incarnation of the divine Wisdom:

Do you not believe that I am in the Father and the Father in me? The words that I say to you I do not speak on my own authority; but the Father who dwells in me does his works. (John 14:10)

Nowhere is this profound relationship between Jesus and his Father more strikingly expressed than in the story of the raising of Lazarus. Just before he performs the miracle, the Johannine Jesus steps aside to engage in prayer with his Father. In what at first sight looks like a put-up job, an offensive piece of exhibitionism, Jesus prays,

Father, I thank thee that thou hast heard

> me. I knew that thou hearest me always,
> but I have said this on account of the
> people standing by, that they may believe
> that thou didst send me. (John 11:41–42)

As Bultmann has commented,[5] the point of this passage is that when Jesus prays vocally he is not engaging in something new but revealing what is going on all the time. He is expressing vocally what he is always doing nonvocally: communing with his Father. He engages in vocal prayer in order to disclose to the bystanders the permanent ground of his life, the basis of his christological significance: "that they may know that thou didst send me." It is because of this that the Johannine Jesus can say, "I and the Father are one" (John 10:30). This is not a dogmatic statement about the substantial unity of the Father and the Son. Rather, it speaks of their unity of purpose, a unity Jesus attains through his life of prayer.

The Johannine Redactor

As we have already noted, the Johannine community was faced with a crisis after the circulation of the Discourse Gospel. With the influx of gentile converts, that Gospel was read in a docetic-gnostic sense. To rule out this misinterpretation, the Redactor introduced a number of additions to the Discourse Gospel. First, he provided it with a prologue, the hymn to the Logos, which was probably already current in the Johannine community. As we have seen, the Discourse Gospel already taught a high Christology of preexistence and incarnation. But it had said nothing about the eternal relationship of the preexistent One to God. Nor did it have anything to say about the activities of the preexistent One. The Logos hymn remedies this deficiency. The Logos, we are told, existed from the beginning ("In the beginning was the Word," John 1:1). He was prior to all creation, as in the Colossians hymn. The Logos shares the being of God himself. He is not inexhaustively identical with God, not all that God was, nor is he another divine being alongside of God. He is the "self-expressive activity of God," that aspect of God's being which is God going out of himself in self-communication: "The Word was God" (*theos*, not *ho theos* and not just *theios*, divine). The Logos was also "with God," i.e., stood in a relationship to God (Greek: *pros*; literally, "toward God"). The Logos was the agent of creation ("All things were made through him," v. 3), as in 1 Cor. 8:6; Col. 1:15–20; and Heb. 1:1–4. The Logos is also—a new point—the agent of ongoing revelation, both to humanity in general ("the life was the light of men," John 1:4; cf. v. 9) and also to Israel in particular ("he came to his own home, and his own people received him not," v. 11). In accordance with the Wisdom tradition, this revelation was often rejected by humanity in general:

The light shines in the darkness,
and the darkness has not overcome it
[v. 5].
. . . yet the world knew him not [v. 10].

The specific revelation to Israel was similarly rejected ("his own people received him not," v. 11). But as in the Wisdom tradition generally, there were some who did receive him:

> But to all who received him,
> who believed in his name,
> he gave power to become children of God.
> (v. 12)

Such people were Abraham, Moses, and the prophets and sages of the past. Then comes the climactic statement:

> And the Word became flesh and dwelt
>   among us,
> full of grace and truth;
> we have beheld his glory,
> glory as of the only Son from the Father.
> (v. 14)

Generations of Anglicans, hearing this text read on Christmas Day, have naturally understood this verse to refer to the birth of Jesus. There is, however, no birth narrative in John's Gospel, as we have seen. Rather, the hymn is spliced into the beginning of the Discourse Gospel, which covers the witness of John the Baptist. That witness speaks first of the future coming of the Messiah (1:26–27) and then of the descent of the dove and the voice from heaven at Jesus' baptism (though it does not narrate the baptism itself, John 1:32–34). From this we would argue that the prologue is intended as a comment on the christological significance, not of Jesus' birth, but of his baptism. This would seem to be clinched by the First Epistle of John, which was perhaps the work of the Redactor himself:

> This is he who came by water and blood,

> Jesus Christ, not with water only, but
> with the water and the blood. (1 John 5:6)

The docetic-gnostics agreed with the "orthodox"
Johannine circle that Jesus Christ came "by
water," that is, that his mission as Revealer of
God was initiated by his baptism. What they
denied and what the author of the Epistle
affirmed was that his death on the cross
("blood") was an integral part of that revelation.
These false teachers believed that the Logos
descended upon Jesus at his baptism and left
him before he died on the cross. But both
orthodox and gnostics agree that the baptism of
Jesus was the primary christological moment.
Does this mean that, for the Johannine
Redactor, the birth was insignificant? Certainly
not. By retaining John 18:37 ("For this was I
born, and for this I have come into the world, to
bear witness to the truth"), the Redactor shows
that the birth was an essential preliminary to
the mission of Jesus, to be the Revealer of God
and to be the incarnation of the divine Wisdom
or Logos. Like the Evangelist, the Redactor
regards the incarnation not as a once-for-all
combination of divinity and humanity, as
abstract substances, at the moment of conception or birth. Rather, it was a process prepared
for at birth, inaugurated in Jesus' Abba
experience at his baptism, and sustained by his
constant communion with the Father. Edwyn
Hoskyns's observation that the word *flesh* in
John 1:14 means "the whole observable history
of Jesus" is thus even more profoundly true
than he realized. But for that observable history
the birth of Jesus was an essential preliminary.

Excursus: Virginal Conception in John?

In speaking of the rebirth of those who accept the Logos, the prologue of John's Gospel describes them as

> . . . children of God, who were born, not of blood nor of the will of the flesh nor of the will of man [Greek: *andros*; literally, "of a male person"], but of God. (John 1:12–13)

There is slight and inferior manuscript evidence (one Old Latin MS, *b*, followed by the Latin version of Irenaeus and by Tertullian) for the reading "who was born" (*qui natus est*). This would make it a direct allusion to the virginal conception of Jesus. Hardly anyone would contend that this was the original reading, although the first edition of the Jerusalem Bible printed it in the text. Yet the reading is significant. The copyist who introduced it perceived that the language about the rebirth of the believers was modeled on the language used for the virginal conception of Jesus. This suggests that the Johannine community was aware of the tradition of the virginal conception, though, as with Jesus' Davidic descent and his birth at Bethlehem, it attaches no christological significance to that tradition.

7. The Birth Stories in Matthew and Luke

In the preceding chapters we have seen how the birth of Jesus played a role, though a minor one, in the kerygma of the early Church and in the Christology of many of the NT writings. Nowhere was there any concern to tell the story of Christ's birth, even in Mark and John, the first and last written Gospels. We have, however, gleaned certain items about the birth of Jesus. He was born of the seed of David. He may or may not have been born at Bethlehem. There was apparently something unusual about his birth, which gave rise to the question of his legitimacy. This unusual circumstance was explained in some circles by the idea of a supernatural conception. In one way or another, the birth could be a significant christological moment, though subordinated to more important moments such as the baptism or, above all, his resurrection. In the Gospels of Matthew and Luke, we encounter for the first time actual narratives of Jesus' birth.

The Traditions behind the Birth Stories

Contemporary scholars identify as pre-Gospel traditions those elements in the birth stories that are common to Matthew and Luke.[1] Despite their irreconcilable differences (e.g., Matthew has Mary and Joseph originally resident at Bethlehem, while Luke places them at Nazareth and moves them to Bethlehem for the birth), they do agree on the following items:

1. The events surrounding the birth occurred in the reign of Herod the Great (Matt. 2:1; Luke 1:5). Since Herod reigned from 37 to 4 B.C., Jesus must have been born in 4 B.C. or earlier.

2. Joseph was considered to be of Davidic descent (Matt. 1:20; Luke 1:27; 2:4).

3. Joseph and Mary were betrothed before the conception of Jesus but came together between the conception and birth (Matt. 1:18, 24; Luke 1:27).[2]

4. Mary became pregnant between betrothal and marriage (Matt. 1:18; Luke 1:34).

5. The pregnancy is interpreted by an angelic annunciation (Matt. 1:18–24; Luke 1:26).

6. This pregnancy was miraculously effected by the operation of the Holy Spirit while Mary was still a virgin (Matt. 1:18; Luke 1:35).

7. The angel directs the child to be named Jesus (Matt. 1:21; Luke 1:31).

8. The angel announces the messianic destiny of the child (Matt. 1:21; Luke 1:32–33, 35; cf. the angelic annunciation to the shepherds at the birth, Luke 2:11).

9. Despite Joseph's not being the father, the child is recognized as being of Davidic descent (Matt. 1:1; Luke 1:32).

10. Jesus is also descended from Abraham (Matt. 1:1, 2, 17; Luke 3:34).

11. Jesus' birth took place after Mary and Joseph came together (Matt. 1:24–25; Luke 2:5).

12. The birth took place at Bethlehem (Matt. 2:1, etc.; Luke 2:4, etc.).

13. A star is connected with the birth of Jesus (Matt. 2:2, 7; Luke 1:78).[3]

14. Jesus' birth was marked by homage done to him by outsiders (Matt. 2:1–12; Luke 2:8–20).

15. Subsequent to the birth, the family took up residence at Nazareth (Matt. 2:23; Luke 2:39).

All of these items call for comment. First, we have to distinguish between those that are historical in nature and those whose motivation is christological. The historical items include items 1 (dating in Herod's reign); 2 (Joseph's Davidic descent); 3 (betrothal and marriage of Mary and Joseph); 11 (birth of Jesus after the marriage of Mary and Joseph). Item 15 (residence at Nazareth) is problematical. It is certainly historical that Jesus was brought up at Nazareth; what is doubtful is whether his parents took up residence there only after his birth. Two other statements are ostensibly historical in nature, but their historicity is debatable. The first is item 4 (the timing of Mary's pregnancy between betrothal and marriage). Raymond Brown has argued strongly for its historicity. For him, it is the basic fact for which the virginal conception through the Holy Spirit provides the theological interpretation.[4] The historicity of this item may be supported by the reports of Jesus' illegitimacy (see above, pp. 76-77 and below, p. 101). On the other hand, the unusual timing of the pregnancy could itself be the product of the christological affirmation of the virginal conception through the Holy Spirit (see below).

Item 12 (location of the birth at Bethlehem) could be historical. We have already noted that Mic. 5:2 does not appear to have been interpreted messianically in pre-Christian Judaism. Also, Matthew does not usually create events to square with prophecy. Similarly, Luke locates the birth at Bethlehem without citing the Micah prophecy. Yet it could equally be an extrapolation from the Davidic Christology along the lines of the discussion in John 7:40–42. We therefore leave the historicity of items 4 (timing of the conception) and 12 (location of birth at Bethlehem) an open question.

Item 9 (Jesus' Davidic descent) is in an ambivalent category. On the one hand, it is, in principle, historical like 2 (Joseph's Davidic descent). That is to say, the family to which they both belonged actually claimed Davidic origin and the claim may have been generally acknowledged (see above, p. 5). On the other hand, from the time of the earliest kerygma (see above, pp. 9-10) the formula "born of the seed of David" always had a christological significance, qualifying Jesus for his later messianic role, and it continues to have this significance in the birth stories. Thus, in Matthew the wise men search for the holy child because he was born "king of the Jews," and they are obviously led to find him at Bethlehem because of its Davidic associations as shown by the Micah prophecy

(Matt. 2:1–6). In Luke's annunciation story, the angel promises to Mary that her child will receive from the Lord "the throne of his father David" (Luke 1:32). Similarly, in the Benedictus, Zechariah welcomes the salvation God is about to raise up "in the house of his servant David" (Luke 1:69).

In one way or another, all the remaining items not covered thus far are intentionally christological in import. The idea behind item 5 (prenatal annunciation) is deeply rooted in the biblical tradition.[5] These annunciations follow a regular pattern:[6] (1) the prospective parents are childless for one reason or another; (2) an angel appears to one of the prospective parents; (3) a reaction of fear at the appearance; (4) reassurance by the angel; (5) the announcement of a birth through a miraculous intervention overcoming the impediment; (6) the announcement of the child's future role in salvation history; (7) the offer of a sign confirming the announcement. In addition to these biblical annunciation stories, certain OT prophets looked back to the moment of their conception or birth as the point at which God predestined them for their prophetic role. Thus Yahweh says to Jeremiah,

Before I formed you in the womb
    I knew you,
And before you were born I
    consecrated you;
I appointed you a prophet to the
    nations. (Jer. 1:5)

In a similar vein the Second Isaiah reports,

The Lord called me from the womb,
    from the body of my mother he

> named my name.
> He made my mouth like a sharp
> sword,
> in the shadow of his hand he hid me;
> he made me a polished arrow,
> in his quiver he hid me away. (Isa. 49:1–2)

Note that everything said about the prophet in connection with his conception or birth is prospective. His mouth is not already at birth a sharp sword. He does not function as a sharp arrow already in the cradle. That will happen later on in life when he assumes his mission as an adult.

That this pattern of prophetic self-understanding was alive in early Christianity is shown by the way the Apostle Paul picks up the same language and applies it to his own mission:

> But when he who had set me apart before I was born [literally, "from my mother's womb," so KJV], and had called me through his grace, was pleased to reveal his Son to me, in order that I might preach him among the Gentiles . . . (Gal. 1:15–16)

In Paul's case, the setting apart in the womb was a preliminary to the apostolic call that came to him on the road to Damascus.

Even more immediately relevant is the annunciation to John the Baptist. Here the angel announces to Zechariah that the son born to him will be the forerunner of the Messiah. That is the role John played later on when he appeared publicly to Israel. True, this role was anticipated in the story of the visitation, when the unborn child leapt in the womb of his

mother to greet the unborn Messiah (Luke 1:44).
But the annunciation itself was referring to the
Baptist's role as an adult. Only then will he

> . . . turn many of the sons
> of Israel to the Lord their God,
> and he will go before him in the
> spirit and power of Elijah,
> to turn the hearts of the fathers to
> the children,
> and the disobedient to the wisdom
> of the just,
> to make ready for the Lord a people prepared.
> (Luke 1:16–17)

It is with a similar prospective reference that we
should interpret the angel Gabriel's two
announcements to Mary. The first runs thus:

> He will be great, and will be called
> the Son of the Most High;
> and the Lord God will give to him
> the throne of his father David,
> and he will reign over the house of
> Jacob for ever;
> and of his kingdom there will be no
> end.
> (Luke 1:32–33)

The second prediction reads as follows:

> The Holy Spirit will come upon
> you,
> and the power of the most high
> will overshadow you;
> therefore the child to be born
> will be called holy,
> the Son of God. . . .
> (Luke 1:35)

The sovereignty and rule of the child to be born are clearly prospective. He will not enter upon his kingly rule until his mission is accomplished on earth. But what of the designation of the child as "Son"? It is often asserted that the word *therefore* in Luke 1:35 implies that the divine sonship is the consequence of the conception through the Holy Spirit, as though the Holy Spirit played the role of an earthly father. That would mean that the conception of Jesus is viewed as the result of a kind of "sacred marriage," as in the pagan legends of gods descending and having intercourse with women to produce demigods.[7] This, however, is to misconstrue what is meant by the title "Son of God" in the synoptic Gospels, where it always designates the role to be played by the figure in question in salvation history. Jesus is "Son of God by appointment"—to use a phrase coined by the late George Caird.[8] That appointment will not take effect until the baptism of Jesus (see Luke 3:22) or possibly even at his exaltation, as in Acts 13:33. The Christology of the virginal conception through the Holy Spirit is similar to that of the sending formula in the pre-Pauline tradition, before Paul had reinterpreted it in terms of preexistence and incarnation (see above, pp. 13-16).

We have included the motif of the star (item 13) among the common elements in the two birth stories. Admittedly, this item is not usually included, and it is employed differently in the two Gospels. In Matthew, a star appears as a sign of Jesus' birth, whereas in Luke, the Benedictus hails the Messiah as himself "the rising star" (Greek: *anatolē*). In the RSV translation, this allusion is lost, for it paraphrases it thus: "the day shall dawn upon us from on high" (Luke 1:78). This, however, obscures the original metaphor of the star that shines brightly before the dawn.[9] It is worth noting that the same Greek word, *anatolē*, occurs in Matt. 2:2, where the RSV translates "we have seen his star *in the East*," but where it is better translated "we have seen his star *at its rising*."[10] The background of these allusions in both Matthew and Luke is in Balaam's prophecy:

> I see him, but not now;
>> I behold him, but not nigh:
> a star shall come forth out of Jacob,
>> and a scepter shall rise out of Israel.
>>>> (Num. 24:17)

Originally, this prediction referred to the rise of the Davidic dynasty. But already in pre-Christian Judaism it had come to be interpreted messianically. It is therefore probable that in the pre-Gospel tradition the birth of Jesus was associated with a rising star, a tradition that found its way in different applications into Matthew and Luke.

Item 14, the homage motif, is common to both Matthew and Luke. Already in the OT, the birth of significant figures in salvation history is an occasion for celebration. Thus, Abraham makes a great feast on the day that Isaac was weaned (Gen. 21:8). After Samuel is weaned, his mother brings him to the house of the Lord in Shiloh and offers sacrifice (1 Sam. 1:24–28). Closer to hand, after John the Baptist was born, Elizabeth's neighbors and kinsfolk, hearing that the Lord had had mercy upon her, came to rejoice with her (Luke 1:58). Since the child born to Mary was destined to be the Messiah, it was appropriate that his birth should be marked by even greater celebration, hence the stories of the magi and the shepherds. In both cases, the motivation is christological. The magi welcome the child as "King of the Jews," while the shepherds are told by the angel that the child now born is "a Savior, who is Christ [Messiah] the Lord" (Luke 2:11). Both stories are narrative expressions of Christology.

We should note that even those items that are historical in origin are narrated solely because of their christological significance. The Davidic descent of Jesus is important only because it qualifies him to be Messiah. The unusual timing of the conception and the location of the birth at Bethlehem (if historical) are recorded only because of their christological significance. The unusual timing gets Joseph out of the way so that room is opened for the Holy Spirit's creative act in bringing Jesus into the world. The birth at Bethlehem indicates that Jesus is the Davidic Messiah.

Basically, there are two Christologies in the birth stories, the Davidic sonship, which makes Jesus eligible for his messianic office, and the divine initiative, which introduced Jesus into history. Take away these Christologies and the birth stories collapse into triviality and meaninglessness.

The Evangelists' Presentation

It is difficult to distinguish between the birth stories as they took shape in the oral tradition and the contribution of the Evangelists themselves. We can, however, identify certain features in which the Evangelists go beyond and add to those elements that we have discerned thus far.

At certain junctures of his narrative, Matthew emphasizes that particular occurrences took place "in order to fulfill what was spoken" by so-and-so the prophet.[11] Such a concern is, of course, in full accord with the earliest kerygma, which asserted that "Christ died for our sins in accordance with the scriptures" (1 Cor. 15:3). Further, many of the pre-Gospel items we discussed above had a basis in the OT. Matthew has, therefore, only systematized what was already implicit in the tradition by means of his fulfillment citations. Second, Matthew introduces a Moses typology into the birth story. The role of Herod and massacre of the innocents recalls the story of Pharaoh and the Hebrew children in Exodus. Again, the flight into Egypt is followed by a return to the Holy Land in which Jesus retraces the steps of Moses. Matthew's Moses typology is a development of the primitive Christian understanding of Jesus' death and resurrection as a new Exodus, and it also prepares the way for the Sermon on the Mount in which Jesus gives the definitive interpretation of the Torah. Third, the role of Herod and the fate of the innocents foreshadows the rejection of Jesus and his ultimate end on the cross.

Turning to Luke, we find that he alone gives narrative expression to the Pauline statement that Christ was "born under the law" (see above, p. 37). This is brought out in the brief narratives of the circumcision of Jesus (Luke 2:21) and of the presentation/purification in the Temple (Luke 2:22–35). Also, consistent with his presentation in the body of the Gospel, Luke depicts Jesus as identified with the poor already in his birth. There was no room for him in the inn (Luke 2:7), and it was shepherds (a despised occupation in contemporary Judaism) who did homage to him at his birth (Luke 2:18–20). Perhaps, too, there is a slight reminiscence of the Pauline statement that Christ "became poor" (2 Cor. 8:9, see above p. 44), though Luke lacks Paul's Christology of preexistence and incarnation at this point ("though he was rich").

Thus, all the redactional features of the birth narratives are either narrative expressions of earlier Christologies or they prepare the way for the Evangelists' own christological presentations in the rest of their Gospels. From start to finish, the birth stories are christological rather than historical in their purpose.

Epilogue: Some Loose Ends

The reader will have noticed that in our discussion of the Christology expressed in the birth stories we said nothing about preexistence/incarnation, not even in connection with the virginal conception.[1] This is all the more surprising when we recall what happened after the NT period. Take, for instance, the Nicene Creed:

> We believe in one Lord, Jesus Christ,
>   the only Son of God,
>   eternally begotten of the Father,
>   God from God, Light from Light,
>   true God from true God,
>   begotten not made,
>   of one Being with the Father;
>   through him all things were made.
>   For us and for our salvation
>   he came down from heaven,
>   was incarnate of the Holy Spirit and the
>   Virgin Mary and became truly human.[2]

Here the loose ends in the Christology of the NT have been tied up: preexistence/incarnation and virginal conception have been synthesized. The same thing has happened in many of our familiar Christmas hymns. Take this, for example:

> Veiled in flesh the God-head see;
> hail the incarnate deity.
> Pleased as man with us to dwell;
> Jesus our Emmanuel.
> . . . .
> Mild he lays his glory by,
> born, that we no more may die,
> born to raise us from the earth,
> born to give us second birth.
> (The Hymnal 1982, no. 87)

Less familiar is the traditional office hymn for the Feast of the Nativity, which has now found a place in the hymnal:

> Behold, the world's creator wears
> the form and fashion of a slave;
> our very flesh our Maker shares,
> his fallen creatures all to save.
> . . . .
> For this how wondrously he wrought!
> A maid in lowly human place
> became, in ways beyond all thought,
> the chosen vessel of his grace.
> (The Hymnal 1982, no. 77)

What has happened in all of these examples is that three different Christologies have been merged together. The Johannine statement, "the Word became flesh," has been interpreted in the light of Paul's Christology of the incarnation of the preexistent Son at birth and applied to the birth of Jesus of a virgin through the Holy Spirit.[3] Now, there is nothing wrong in principle with this combination of various Christologies, for that was already happening in the NT. Paul, for instance, combined Jesus' Davidic descent with the sending Christology to produce a pattern of preexistence/incarnation (see above, pp. 33-34). Similarly, the birth stories combine Davidic descent with historical sending.[4] Unfortunately, however, in the process the distinctive characteristics of the various Christologies have become blurred. Paul's insistence that the preexistent One surrendered the divine glory and took the form of a servant or slave has been obscured. Hebrews' insistence that the Christ had to learn obedience through suffering fell into oblivion. The Fourth Gospel's dynamic view of the incarnation as a reality achieved not once for all at birth but actuated continuously through Jesus' Abba experience and his constant communion with the Father was forgotten. We cannot insist too strongly that the preexistence of the eternal Son did not give the incarnate One any advantage over the rest of us. Jesus, like us, had to start from scratch. He did not know everything in advance as a result of his divine origin. Nor was he exempted in advance from ignorance, temptation, and sin. The dogma of preexistence and incarnation is not a presupposition of Jesus' history. It is a confession of faith we come to at the end of it, when we have encountered in the history of this very human Jesus "God's presence and his very self" (*The Hymnal 1982*, no. 445).

Notes

Chapter 1. Jesus' Attitude to His Own Birth

1. It has sometimes been argued that the unusual designation "son of Mary" betrays Mark's knowledge of Jesus' virginal conception and thus of a tradition that was later included in the birth stories. Others have held that the designation reflects the popular Jewish supposition of Jesus' illegitimacy, which in turn may reflect the facticity of the virginal conception. The Lutheran-Catholic task force rejected both these interpretations. We preferred instead to understand "son of Mary" to imply Joseph's early demise: Jesus was "Mary's boy from down the street." See Raymond E. Brown et al., eds., *Mary in the New Testament* (Philadelphia: Fortress; New York: Paulist, 1978), 61–68.

2. Q is the symbol used to designate the material common to Matthew and Luke but not found in Mark (though there is an overlap between Mark and Q). The designation Q is derived from the German *Quelle*, according to the usual explanation.

3. Stage 1 materials are those authentic to the earthly Jesus; stage 2 represents oral tradi-

tion originating in the post-Easter community; and stage 3, the Evangelists' redaction. These useful designations of the three levels of tradition in the Gospels were formulated by an instruction of the Pontifical Biblical Commission of the Roman Catholic Church, "Instruction on the Historical Truth of the Gospels" (April 24, 1964), reprinted in Latin and English, *CBQ* 26 (1964), 299–312.

4. The three passages (Mark 10:46–52; 11:1–10; and 12:35–37a) will be treated as stage 2 materials in chapter 3.

5. I have discussed this question in *The Mission and Achievement of Jesus* (London: SCM, 1954), 114–15. A similar position with regard to Jesus' Davidic descent is taken by E. Schweizer, *The Good News According to Mark* (Atlanta: Knox, 1970), ad loc.: "The origin of this concept can be explained here only if Jesus' family actually did trace its lineage back to David and if the church knew this fact but neither denied it nor covered it up."

Chapter 2. The Birth of Christ in the Earliest Communities

1. This is the position adopted by Eduard Schweizer in his essay "Concerning the Speeches in Acts," in Leander E. Keck and J. Louis Martyn, eds., *Studies in Luke-Acts: Essays in Honor of Paul Schubert* (Nashville/New York: Abingdon, 1966), 208–16. To my mind, this is the most convincing answer to a much-debated question.

2. On the sending formula, see Werner Kramer, *Christ, Lord, Son of God* (SBT 50; London: SCM, 1966), 111–15.

Chapter 3. The Birth of Christ in Mark and Q

1. This statement needs some qualification. There are some thirty sayings found in both Mark and Q, but the Q versions occur in non-Marcan contexts in Matthew and Luke or where, in the case of Matthew, Mark and Q versions are conflated. A minority of American and British scholars have questioned the two-source theory and the necessity of the Q hypothesis, but their views have failed to convince the majority of scholars.

2. Mark says that the heavens were "torn apart" (Greek: *schizomenous*) at the descent of the dove. Matthew and Luke say they were "opened" (Matthew: *aneōchthēsan*; Luke: *aneōchthēnai*). This difference is obscured by RSV, which translates "opened" in all three Gospels.

3. Eduard Schweizer has recently noted the affinity between Q's Wisdom Christology and the incarnational Christology of the hymns in John 1:1–18 and Phil. 2:6–11. See E. Schweizer, *Theologische Einleitung zum Neuen Testament* (Neues Testament Deutsch, Supplement 2; Göttingen: Vandenhoeck & Ruprecht, 1989), 43–44. There is, however, an important difference between Q and the Logos hymn. Q is interested only in the revelatory functions of Wisdom and not, like John 1:1–18, in Wisdom's creative activity.

Chapter 4. Paul: Preexistence and Incarnation

1. The generally accepted letters, the so-called homologoumena, are 1 Thessalonians,

Galatians, 1 and 2 Corinthians, Philippians, Philemon, and Romans. The deutero-Paulines, or antilegomena, are Colossians, Ephesians, and the Pastorals (1 and 2 Timothy, Titus). The second group provides evidence for the "reception" of Paul in the subsequent generation. While the church accepts them as canonical Scripture and as part of the Pauline corpus, they cannot be used as historical evidence for the theology of Paul himself.

2. By Martin Dibelius in his essay "Jungfrauensohn und Krippenkind," reprinted in his collected essays, *Botschaft und Geschichte* (Tübingen: Mohr, 1953), 1:1–78.

3. See Peter Stuhlmacher, "Recent Exegesis on Romans 3:24–26," in *Reconciliation, Law, & Righteousness: Essays in Biblical Theology* (Philadelphia: Fortress, 1986), 94–109.

4. Philo, *Leg. All.* 2. 86.

5. See above, n. 3.

6. Michael Goulder, "Two Roots of the Christian Myth," in John Hick, ed., *The Myth of God Incarnate* (Philadelphia: Westminster, 1977), 64–86.

7. Harold W. Attridge, *Hebrews*, Hermeneia —A Critical and Historical Commentary on the Bible (Philadelphia: Fortress, 1989), 79–82.

Chapter 5. Incarnational Christology after Paul

1. In the Greek, *he* is represented by a relative pronoun, *who.*

2. For a good discussion on the situation presupposed by Ephesians, see David G. Meade,

Pseudonymity and Canon (Grand Rapids, MI: Eerdmans, 1986), 142–48.

3. For the chiastic structure of 1 Tim. 3:16, see Reginald H. Fuller, *The Foundation of New Testament Christology* (New York: Scribner's, 1965), 216–17.

4. Eduard Schweizer, *Theologische Einleitung in das Neue Testament* (Neues Testament Deutsch, Supplement 2; Göttingen: Vandenhoeck & Ruprecht, 1989), 35. (English translation by R. H. Fuller.)

5. See Harold W. Attridge, *Hebrews*, Hermeneia—A Critical and Historical Commentary on the Bible (Philadelphia: Fortress, 1989), 50–62.

Chapter 6. The Johannine Writings

1. In his posthumously published Bampton lectures, the late John A. T. Robinson contended that John's Gospel in its entirety represents a "lower" Christology. See John A. T. Robinson, *The Priority of John* (London: SCM, 1985; Oak Park, IL: Meyer Stone, 1987), 343–97. A distinction must, however, be drawn between the different strata in the Johannine discourses. The Christology of the earlier stratum is "low," and that of the later discourse material is "high."

2. Robinson passes over these passages too easily and does not face up to the difficulty of interpreting them in terms of a "lower" Christology.

3. Robinson, *Priority*, 371.

4. The present writer, following an earlier

suggestion of Alfred Loisy, the famous French Catholic Modernist, tentatively proposed that for John's Gospel the baptism of Jesus was the moment of the incarnation. See Reginald H. Fuller, "Christmas, Epiphany and the Johannine Prologue," in Madeleine L'Engle and William B. Green, eds., *Spirit and Light: Essays in Historical Theology* (In Honor of Edward N. West; New York: Seabury, 1976), 63–73. This proposal has since been taken up favorably and developed independently by Piet Schoonenberg in his Bellarmine lecture, "A Sapiential Reading of John's Prologue: Some reflections on the views of Reginald Fuller and James Dunn," *Theology Digest* 32 (1986), 403–20; and by Francis Watson, "Is John's Christology Adoptionist?" in L. D. Hurst and N. T. Wright, eds., *The Glory of Christ in the New Testament: Studies in Christology* (In Memory of George Caird; Oxford: Clarendon, 1987), 13–24. Neither of these writers pays sufficient attention to John 18:37, which shows that the birth of Jesus did have a christological significance for John, albeit a preparatory one.

5. Rudolf Bultmann, *The Gospel of John: A Commentary* (Philadelphia: Westminster, 1971), 402–9. Bultmann writes, "He [Jesus] does not need to be quickened out of a prayerless attitude to make petition by reason of a particular situation."

Chapter 7. The Birth Stories in Matthew and Luke

1. Agreements between the two birth stories are listed in Raymond E. Brown, SS, *The Birth*

of the Messiah (Garden City, NY: Doubleday, 1977), 34–35; Joseph A. Fitzmyer, SJ, *The Gospel According to Luke: Introduction, Translation, and Notes*, I-IX. (Garden City, NY: Doubleday, 1981), 307. Brown gives eleven items; Fitzmyer, twelve. The list given above includes additional items.

2. Curiously, Luke says they were still only betrothed when they traveled together to Bethlehem. But given the social conventions of the time, their being together would require that they were married. Later copyists spotted the inconsistency and sought to remove it by adding "wife" after "betrothed" (see KJV *ad loc.*). This merely replaces one anomaly by another.

3. For the interpretation of *anatolē* in Luke 1:78 as "rising star," see below, pp. 92-93.

4. See Brown, *Birth*, 517–31. Surprisingly, Brown rejects the evidence for the slander of illegitimacy, thus weakening his case for the historicity of the unusual timing of Mary's pregnancy.

5. Annunciation stories occur prior to the conception/birth of the following OT figures: Isaac (to the prospective father, Abraham, Gen. 17:1–8); Samson (to the prospective mother, Judg. 13:2–7). Similar annunciations are provided for John the Baptist in the NT (to the prospective father, Zechariah, Luke 1:8–24) and in the NT Apocrypha for Mary, Mother of Jesus (to Anna, her prospective mother, *Protevangelium Iacobi* 4, 1; English translation in Edgar Hennecke, *New Testament Apocrypha* [ed. Wilhelm Schneemelcher and trans. ed. R. McL. Wilson; Philadelphia: Westminster, 1963], 373) and to

Mary's prospective father, Joachim (*ibid.*, 4, 2). These last two examples are instructive as showing the contemporary milieu in which the annunciations of Jesus were created, as well as the purpose of their creation, viz., to foreshadow the role to be played by Jesus in salvation history.

6. The full annunciation pattern is set out in Brown, *Birth*, 156, table 8. It contains thirteen items, not all of which appear in any given annunciation.

7. The alleged pagan parallels are conveniently tabulated in T. Boslooper, *The Virgin Birth* (Philadelphia: Westminster, 1962), 135–86. He offers parallels from Buddhist, Hindu, Egyptian and Greco-Roman religions.

8. George B. Caird, "Son by Appointment," in William C. Weinrich, ed., *The New Testament Age*; Essays in Honor of Bo Reicke (Macon, GA: Mercer, 1984), 1:73–78.

9. Fitzmyer, *Luke*, 1:387, notes "rising Star" as a possible meaning of *anatolē* in this place, though he does not favor it.

10. So Brown, *Birth*, *ad loc.*

11. The fulfillment citations in Matthew's infancy narrative are Matt. 1:23 – Isa. 7:14 (virginal conception); 2:5 – Mic. 5:1–3 (Bethlehem as place of birth); 2:15 – Hos. 11:1 (return from Egypt placed by anticipation at the prior journey to Egypt); 2:18 – Jer. 31:15 (slaughter of the innocents); 2:23 – ? (residence at Nazareth). Unlike the christological items, the fulfillment citations are tacked on externally to the narratives and are not constitutive of them.

Epilogue: Some Loose Ends

1. The absence of a Christology of pre-existence/incarnation from the infancy narratives and, in particular, the fact that the virginal conception is not designed to express such a Christology has been convincingly argued by Brown, *Birth,* 140–42. Some scholars even contend with some justification that the very idea of virginal conception through the Holy Spirit excludes preexistence, involving as it does an act of creation *ex nihilo.*

2. Translation from *Prayer Book Studies 30* (New York: Hymnal Corporation, 1989), 61. The translation of the clause referring to the conception is an improvement on that in *The Book of Common Prayer* (1979).

3. Preexistence/incarnation Christology is already combined with the virginal conception in Ignatius of Antioch. Compare, e.g., "for our God, Jesus the Christ, was conceived in the womb of Mary according to a dispensation of the seed of David but also of the Holy Ghost" (Ignatius, *Ephesians* 16) with "Jesus Christ, who was with the Father before the worlds and appeared at the end of time" (*idem, Magnesians* 6).

4. The Davidic descent is in ostensible conflict with the virginal conception since it depends on Joseph's physical paternity. We are here dealing with two different Christologies, not with irreconcilable historical traditions.

Index

77828